Psychology and Crime

Kevin Brewer

Heinemann Educational Publishers
Halley Court, Jordon Hill, Oxford, OX2 8EJ
a division of Reed Educational & Professional Publishing Ltd

OXFORD MELBOURNE AUKLAND
JOHANNESBURG BLANTYRE GABORONE
IBADAN PORTSMOUTH NH(USA) CHICAGO

Text © Kevin Brewer, 2000
First published in 2000

04 03 02 01 00
9 8 7 6 5 4 3 2 1

British Library Cataloguing in Publication Data
A catalogue record for this book is available from the British Library

ISBN 0 435 80653X

Typeset by Wyvern 21 Ltd, Bristol
Picture research by Thelma Gilbert
Illustration by Paul Beebee at Beehive Illustration
Printed and bound in Great Britain by The Bath Press Ltd, Bath

Acknowledgements
The authors and publishers would like to thank the following for the use of copyright material: HMSO for the table from *Annual Abstract of Statistics*, 1999 on p. 1; for the table and extract from the *1996 British Crime Survey* on pp. 2 and 78; for the table from the *1998 British Crime Survey* on p. 52; for the table from *Memorandum of Good Practice on Video Interviews with Child Witnesses for Criminal Proceedings*, Home Office, 1992 on p. 71. Crown Copyright is reproduced with the permission of the Controller of Her Majesty's Stationery Office; Federal Bureau of Investigation for the table from 'Crime scene and profile characteristics of organized and disorganized murders', *FBI Law Enforcement Bulletin 54*, vol. 8, 1985, pp. 18–25 on p. 38.

The publishers would like to thank the following for permission to use photographs: Telegraph Colour Library on p. 9; Popperfoto on pp. 23 and 24; Associated Press on p. 29 and Solo Syndication on p. 39.

Cover photograph by AKG London

The publishers have made every effort to trace the copyright holders, but if they have inadvertently overlooked any, they will be pleased to make the necessary arrangements at the first opportunity.

Tel: 01865 888058 www.heinemann.co.uk

C) Contents

1) **Introduction**

The application of psychology to specific areas like crime, health or education is a relatively new phenomena. Thus it is often unclear what the boundaries of each particular application are. The application of psychology to crime can be found in the library under different headings such as 'Criminal psychology', 'Criminological psychology', 'Legal psychology' and 'Forensic psychology'.

There is often overlap with sociology and criminology. But whatever the name, the common pattern is the application of psychology to understanding crime and the legal process. So altogether we are talking about the application of psychology to a number of individuals – police and legal officers, criminals, witnesses and victims. This book is divided into four chapters, with each chapter looking at one of these groups of individuals.

Chapter 1

This chapter is concerned with the investigators of crime (that is, the police). First it asks whether it's possible to say how much crime actually takes place. Then it looks at the investigators (is there a certain type of 'police personality'?), and how the police go about interviewing the suspects.

Chapter 2

Here we concentrate on the criminals themselves, asking why do some individuals break the law while others do not. Is there something different about criminals compared to non-criminals? If there is such a difference, does it help in their capture, through the use of offender profiling?

Chapter 3

In this chapter we look at the witnesses and the accuracy of their recall of events, and at the victims of crime. Often the witnesses and victims are the same people.

Chapter 4

The final chapter is concerned with the legal system and asks whether psychology can be applied to what is happening in the court room, in particular to the jury. Then it looks at what sort of punishment is appropriate and whether society should be trying to rehabilitate offenders instead.

How to use this book

This book has a number of features to help you understand the topic more easily. It is written to give you a wide range of skills in preparation for any of the new AS and A level psychology syllabi. Below is a list of the features with a brief summary to explain how to use them.

1 Real Life Applications

These consist of 'text boxes' that develop further a concept already discussed within the main text. Often they provide articles or outlines of studies. In all cases they attempt to apply theory to 'real life situations'.

2 Commentary

These paragraphs appear throughout the book. They follow on from issues raised within the main text. They serve a number of functions: to provide an evaluation of the earlier text, to clarify a point or to highlight some related issue. Sometimes they provide 'for' and 'against' debates.

3 Key studies

As the title implies these are descriptions of important studies within a specific area. There are two of these for each chapter. They briefly identify the aims, method, results and conclusions of the study. This feature helps you to understand the methodology of research.

4 Questions

Each 'Real Life Application' has two or three short answer questions designed to test a range of skills including summarising, outlining and evaluating. All of these activities are designed to allow you to acquire the 'study skills' outlined within the syllabi. In addition, two or three 'essay-style' questions are included at the end of each chapter. They relate specifically to the material covered within the chapter.

5 Advice on answering questions

There is a short section at the end of this book that gives brief advice on answering all the essay questions. It also provides answers to the short questions presented in this book.

1 Crime and the police

This chapter tackles two main themes: the measurement of crime (what it is and how much takes place) and the police (including whether there is a certain type of person who joins the police force). Real Life Applications that are considered are:

- RLA 1: Police 'action man' image
- RLA 2: Can you tell if someone is lying?
- RLA 3: False confession and Carole Richardson
- RLA 4: Serial false confessor

The most obvious definition of 'criminal behaviour' is that it's any behaviour that violates criminal law, whether the offender is caught or not. But what is classed as criminal will vary between countries and at different historical times. For example, the age of criminal responsibility is eight years old in Scotland, but fifteen in Sweden (Hollin, 1992). Criminal behaviour can be different to anti-social or morally offensive behaviour. The issue of 'recreational drugs' shows that something can be criminal but not necessarily morally offensive for many people. Some people view fox-hunting as morally offensive, but it is not criminal behaviour at this stage.

How much crime is there?

Table 1.1: Notifiable offences recorded by the police in England and Wales in thousands

Offence	1987	1997
Violence against the person	141.0	250.8
Sexual offences	25.2	33.2
Burglary	900.1	1015.1
Robbery	32.6	63.1
Theft and handling stolen goods	2052.0	2165.0
Fraud and forgery	133.0	134.4
Criminal damage	589.0	877.0
Other offences	19.3	59.8
Total	3892.2	4598.4

Source: *Annual Abstract of Statistics,* 1999.

The most obvious answer to this question is to look at the official statistics collected by the Home Office in Britain from police records (see Table 1.1). The police definitions of crime are based on certain criteria: usually incidents that have reasonable evidence for their existence and could be punished by a court. But the police records are not necessarily an accurate measure of the amount of crime that takes place. This is due to a number of facts about police recording of crime.

- A crime may not be reported by the victims (see reasons for this in Chapter 3), or the victims may withdraw their charges. This latter case is written off as 'no crime', and Sparks *et al* (1977) found that nearly one-third of initial reports were subsequently categorized this way in a London study.
- Human error in misrecording the crime.
- The police can make the decision as to whether to include a crime in the figures. They may feel that there is an error in the report or a lack of evidence.
- The police may use discretion or be under pressure about certain crimes. Police forces can also vary from region to region in their prosecution of particular crimes. Farrington and Dowds (1985) found that the methods used by Nottinghamshire police to record crime made it appear the most crime-ridden area in the country.
- The appearance of the police may resolve an issue, and a crime is not committed (for example, the police appearance at a dispute may stop any potential violence).
- Increased reporting of incidents in recent years because of increased telephones generally, and mobile phones.

- The time between the crime and reporting it to the police does not allow investigation (that is, many years may have passed).

Alternatives to the official statistics

Based on the reports of a sample of victims, comparison can be made with the official records of crime. For some crimes, the level of reporting is high (around 90% for car thefts), but lower on other cases (around one-third of robberies are reported). There are problems with self-reported victim surveys like the British Crime Survey.

- The respondent could make up an offence.
- The respondent could misunderstand the question and give incorrect information.
- The answers could include an incident not in the appropriate time period for the survey.
- The respondent could forget an incident.
- There are sampling problems – from who to choose in the sample to how to multiply the sample results to give a total figure for the population. (Details of the sampling for the British Crime Survey are discussed in Chapter 3.)

Data from the British Crime Surveys are not always directly comparable with the police figures (see Table 1.2, below)

Table 1.2: Comparison of British Crime Survey and police figures

British Crime Survey	Police figures
Since 1982: reported and unreported crime.	Since 1876: offences that can be tried in court.
Independent of changes in police recording.	Good measure of police workload.
Does not measure well at small area level.	Data at level of 43 police forces.
Does not include crime involving under 16s, common assaults commercial crime, crime involving those in institutions, 'victimless crime' (for example, drug abuse), fraud, sexual offences, murder and manslaughter.	Does include crime involving under 16s, common assaults, commercial crime, crime involving those in institutions, 'victimless crime', fraud, sexual offences, murder and manslaughter.
Collects details of crime.	Collects details of the arrest.

Comparable figures between British Crime Survey and police figures

Burglary.	Theft of/from motor vehicle.
Bicycle theft.	Theft from persons.
Incidents of vandalism.	Wounding.
Robbery	

Non-comparable figures

Non-burglary household thefts.	Common assault.
Thefts of personal property.	

Source: adapted from Mirrlees-Black *et al*, 1996.

Offender surveys

These are surveys based on a sample of individuals with a criminal record.

Using a sample of 137 male sexual offenders, Groth *et al* (1982) asked them about the number of sexual offences committed. Their confidentiality was assured. The researchers found many undetected offences – an average of five for each offender. This suggests that sexual offences could be severely under-recorded by the police.

An alternative method is to ask individuals without criminal records if they have committed undetected offences. Furnham and Thompson (1991) found that 88% of undergraduates asked had drunk alcohol under the age of sixteen, and 74% had viewed an '18' certificate film under age. Most of the offences were trivial, with only 1% admitting to theft. However, there is always the question as to whether these types of self-reported surveys are accurate. Individuals could exaggerate or not admit to some crimes.

Police and the interview process

Traditionally the police have had no formal training in interviewing suspects, and learn from watching others or using their own feelings.

Commentary

Baldwin (1993) analysed 600 recorded interviews and found the quality of interview varied. Baldwin argued that 218 interviews were poor quality, due to general ineptitude and lack of planning, an assumption of guilt leading to repetitive questions, too much pressure exerted on the witness, or excessive interruptions.

Real Life Application 1:

Police 'action man' image

After the miscarriages of justices with the Guildford Four (see pages 6, 7), the Association of Chief Police Officers is reviewing the interview training of police officers.

The police often use unethical methods which are based on charisma and presence; what is called in police canteen culture 'making a psychological impact'.

Professor Geoffrey Stephenson of the University of Kent says that police interviewers find it difficult to deal with assertive interviewees, or those who do not answer the questions. He carried out research at 10 London police stations with over 1000 cases of interrogation. In 73% of the cases, officers were certain of the suspect's guilt before the interview. 'Officers in most of the cases saw an interview as a means of obtaining a confession rather than an opportunity to gather information.'

Source: adapted from the *Daily Telegraph*, 1991.

Summary

- Because many of the police officers believed in the suspect's guilt before the interview, they saw the interview as a means of gaining a confession. This could involve methods that were legally unacceptable called by the police 'making a psychological impact'.

Questions

1 How do the findings of Stephenson link to the research of Pearse and Gudjonsson (1999)?

2 In how many interviews were the police sure of the suspect's guilt beforehand?

3 What type of interviewees do the police find difficult to deal with?

Types of people interviewed

The police are involved in interviewing four types of people: victims, witnesses, complainants (those who report the crime) and suspects. The first three can, in fact, be the same person. Witnesses and complainants could also be suspects. Depending on the person, the style of the interview will vary. Gudjonsson (1992) divides the standard police interview into four phases.

- Phase 1, 'Orientation': here the purpose of the interview is outlined, the participants are introduced and any legal requirements fulfilled (like cautioning a suspect). If the individual is not sure whether they are a witness or a suspect, this can influence the testimony given.
- Phase 2, 'Listening': the interviewee recounts the events.
- Phase 3, 'Questions and answers': the police ask specific questions based on the information provided in Phase 2.
- Phase 4, 'Advice': the interview is concluded, and any legal requirements fulfilled (for example, signing a written statement).

Commentary

The biggest problem, beside getting information about the event, is that of leading questions. A leading question indicates the wanted answer. For example: 'We have arrested the person who committed the crime. Do you recognize the criminal in the identity parade?' This can be rephrased to avoid leading as: 'We have arrested someone who may or may not have committed the crime. Do you recognize anybody in the identity parade as the criminal?'

Purpose of the interview

The purpose of the interview is to gain as much information as possible. Gorden (1975) highlights potential inhibitors to effective communication in the interview. Some of the inhibitors relate to the unwillingness of the interviewee to give information. Issues here include privacy or threat to self-esteem. Other inhibitors are concerned with the inability to give information. These relate to the interviewee's state of mind.

Gorden argues that these inhibitors can be overcome by facilitators by the police interviewers. These include recognition of the interviewee's need for approval to enhance their self-esteem, and sympathetic understanding as the interviewee has the need to be understood and accepted.

The interviewee may also use deception ('other-deception' – Gudjonsson, 1990), and self-deception. The use of deception may be in terms of the information given in the interview or in terms of the impression they give in the interview. Gudjonsson (1990) found that violent and sex offenders attempted to show respect and consideration for others more than other groups of offenders.

Victims, witnesses and complainants may also use deception. All these people are also involved in impression management.

Commentary

Concerning self-deception, many suspects are employing denial mechanisms (even after being found guilty). Salter (1988) noted that sex offenders have a number of levels of denial – denial of the offences, denial of the planning of the offences, denial of responsibility for the offence and denial of the seriousness of the behaviour.

Real Life Application 2:

Can you tell if someone is lying?

There is a popular belief that liars give themselves away in different ways. But research shows that spotting who is lying is far from easy. Graham Davies addresses three possible ways of catching liars. First, non-verbal clues like blinking more, longer hesitations, higher speech pitch and more speech errors. These accompany lying, but they are also signs of stress. The same is true with what is called 'non-verbal leakage' (for example, foot-tapping). Second, 'micro-expressions' like minute smiles. Unfortunately these can only be spotted by analysing a video frame by frame. Lastly, the use of polygraphs. Davies argues that these can be beaten and are often used by untrained operators. They tend to make false-positive mistakes (that is, they believe the person is lying when telling the truth). The answer to telling if people are lying is to listen to what is actually said.

Source: *All in the Mind*, 1991.

Summary

- The non-verbal signs of whether a person is lying are ambiguous and could also appear if a person is stressed.

Questions

1 How effective is the use of the polygraph compared to observing the individual?
2 Which is a better way of spotting a liar – non-verbal or verbal clues?
3 What is a polygraph?

Giving statements

When interviewees give statements to the police, there are two types of error that can occur: unintended errors (this is a question of accuracy of recall of information) or intentional deception (known as credibility). The credibility of the statement can be assessed in a number of ways.

- By analysis of the content of the statement (for example, whether it is logically consistent). More sophisticated techniques have been developed to analyse the content of the statement. One technique is known as stylometry. This is a technique used in other areas, like history or literature, to identify the author of a particular document by looking at the individual's style of writing or speaking. Osgood (1960), for example, was able to distinguish between genuine and non-genuine suicide notes using this technique. Stylometry has been found to reliably discriminate between truthful and untruthful statements. There is also Statement Validity Assessment (SVA) and Criteria-Based Content Analysis (CBCA). These make use of other information like the fact that recall of real events is very different from fabricated ones.
- The way the statement is presented verbally (for example, speech rate). There is some evidence that when lying, people use longer speech hesitations, and more speech and grammatical errors. But this is only a weak link.
- The accompanying non-verbal behaviour with the statement.
- The use of psychophysiological measures like the polygraph. The polygraph measures physiological responses like heart rate, blood pressure and galvanic skin response. The assumption is that these indicators can show if the person is lying.

Commentary

Unfortunately, the polygraph only measures arousal, which can occur other than when the person is lying. The use of evidence from a polygraph is not admissible in England, but it is in some states in the USA.

Using polygraphs

There are two main techniques used with polygraphs: the Control Question Technique (CQT) is based on comparing the responses to relevant and irrelevant questions using 'Yes' and 'No' answers; the Guilty Knowledge Technique (GKT) uses multiple-choice questions to establish if the suspect is concealing information that only the offender would know.

However, it is possible to 'beat' the polygraph by thinking about excitable things during the neutral questions, thereby making the baseline similar to the critical questions. This is known as 'boosting the baseline'. Alternatively, it is possible to create 'simulated lies' by tensing the toes, for example.

There are many studies that examine the accuracy of the use of polygraphs, and often, in experiments, it is found that the level of accuracy is similar to good observation of the individual. Ginton *et al* (1982 – quoted in Carroll, 1991) used Israeli police officers in an experiment about cheating on a maths test. There were thirteen innocent officers. Just from observing the officers during an interview, eleven were judged innocent and two guilty. However, using the polygraph produced three guilty, seven innocent and three unsure.

Can individuals estimate correctly the credibility of statements? Studies found a hit rate of between 45% and 60% (with chance being 50%). So the hit rate is not that good, but individuals overestimate their ability. There is no difference between experienced or inexperienced individuals, nor does training improve the hit rate.

Context of the interview

The simple fact of being interviewed by the police for whatever reason can be anxiety-producing. But for suspects detained for 24 hours or longer, it can be physically exhausting and emotionally disturbing.

Often the police assume that nervousness during this time is a sign of guilt. But innocent suspects can feel anxious because of fear of being wrongly assumed guilty, of the experience of detention, or that the police may discover private details about them (Inbau *et al*, 1986).

Irving and Hilgendorf (1980) list three groups of stressors experienced by suspects.

- The physical environment of the police station, including the uncertainty and lack of control while there.
- Confinement and isolation from friends and family.
- The power of the authority figures (that is, the police).

The suspect's confession

Suspects may confess during the police interview in a number of ways: a direct admission to the charges made, self-incriminating admission but not a full confession, or confession to other 'unsolved' offences.

Studies in England find that the number of suspects who confess during the police interview varies between 42% and 76%. For example, Mitchell (1983) using the Worcester Crown Court files of 1978 found that 71% of suspects fully confessed to the offence and another 14% made self-incriminating admissions. But this study was only based on those suspects who were committed to trial. The focus of the research has been to establish whether certain types of suspect confess more than others. Gudjonsson (1992) summarizes the main findings.

- Younger suspects are more likely to confess than older ones. Softley (1980) found that 53% of suspects over 21 years old made confessions or self-incriminating admissions compared to 68% of those younger than 21. The difference may be due to younger suspects not being so 'psychologically equipped' for the interview, and/or less aware of their legal rights. Older suspects more often used the right to silence if the evidence against them was strong (Moston *et al*, 1992).
- There are differences in the rates of confession depending on the type of offence: more confessions for property offences (for example, theft) than non-property (for example, violent offences), and more from sex offenders than non-sex offenders (89.3% versus 52.5% respectively – Mitchell, 1983). The differences may be due to the availability of forensic evidence to support the police case.
- Suspects with previous convictions make fewer confessions than first-time offenders (59% versus 76% for first-time offenders – Softley, 1980). However, Mitchell (1983) did find the opposite. This finding could be due to the past experiences of the police interview.

Based on work in Iceland, Gudjonsson and Petursson (1991) note three factors involved in the decision to confess or not: 'internal pressure' (for example, feelings of guilt), 'external pressure' (for example, pressure from police), and the amount of proof that suspects believe the police have found. The last factor seems to be the most powerful, and 55% of the suspects said they confessed because of the evidence against them.

Some suspects will not confess even when the evidence against them is strong. In this case, the police will introduce new tactics in order to gain a confession. Based on the tapes of eighteen interviews of serious criminal cases, Pearse and Gudjonsson (1999) noted that the police interviewers may resort to intimidation, robust challenges and manipulation to gain a confession. But in 22% of cases such tactics led to inadmissible evidence.

Commentary: For and against – theories of confession

Cognitive-behavioural model of confession
Confession is viewed in terms of 'antecedents' and 'perceived consequences'. Antecedents (A) are triggers to confessing as opposed to the short-term (S) and long-term (L) consequences of the confession.
A = social – for example, police pressure; S = police approval; L = punishment.
A = emotional – for example, distress; S = relief; L = guilt.
A = cognitive – for example, thinking that police know; S = thinking good to get off chest; L = uncertainty of future.
A = situational – for example, nature of arrest; S = access to solicitor; L = judicial proceedings.
A = physiological – for example, fear; S = reduction in fear; L =arousal normal.

Source: Gudjonsson, 1992.

Interaction process model of confession (Moston et al, 1992)
Suspect's response to questions influenced by, first, background characteristics (BC) of the suspect and the offence and, second, contextual characteristics (CC) of the case. It is the interaction of both these factors and the subsequent interaction with the police interviewer that produces the confession or not.
BC = gender of supect; CC = strength of evidence.
BC = personality of supect; CC = interview techniques.
BC = type of offence.
BC = severity of offence.

False confessions

Just because a suspect confesses to the offence, it does not mean he or she actually did it, as the example RLA 3 shows (see next column).

Real Life Application 3:

False confession and the Carole Richardson case

On 5 October 1974, IRA bombs destroyed two pubs in Guildford killing five people and injuring many more. Carole Richardson was arrested on 3 December and questioned until 12 December. She had taken a large dose of barbiturates on the first day of questioning.

During the questioning she confessed to planting one of the bombs, but later retracted the confession. As the questioning continued, she became more distressed, but was not given access to a solicitor until 11 December. Unable to notify anybody about the arrest, she confessed out of fear. It was enforced by the police confidence of her guilt and their full control of the situation. With time Carole came to believe that she was a bomber because she could not remember what she was doing on 5 October.

Carole Richardson was found guilty in 1975, but it was not until 20 years later that her conviction was declared a miscarriage of justice.

Source: Gudjonsson, 1992.

Summary

- The case of Carole Richardson shows how an ordinary person kept in custody and questioned heavily by the police can come to believe that he or she did commit the crime. Carole was not able to see her diary to remind her where she was on the day of the bombings. She had also taken a large dose of barbiturates on the first day of questioning.

Questions

1 Why did it matter that Carole could not tell anybody about her arrest?
2 What are the two key factors in her false confession?
3 What type of false confession did she make?

Types of false confession

Kassin and Wrightsman (1985) suggest three types of false confession.

- Voluntary – individuals voluntarily go to the

police to confess, and there is no police pressure. The reasons include a need for attention, strong general feelings of guilt, the inability to distinguish fact from fantasy or a desire to protect the real offender.

- Coerced-compliant – individuals confess because of the pressure during the interview. The pressure may involve the belief that they will be allowed to go home after confessing, or meeting the implicit demands of the interview. The suspect still knows they did not commit the crime.

- Coerced-internalized – suspects come to believe during the interview that they did commit the offence. This phenomena is based on 'memory distrust syndrome', where the individual starts to doubt their own memory of events (Gudjonsson and MacKeith, 1982). Alternatively the suspect may have amnesia at the beginning of the interview.

Gudjonsson (1995) reports the case of Mr J who confessed to arson while working as a volunteer fire officer. Four factors combined to explain his 'coerced-internalized' false confession: an eagerness to please the police, trust and respect for the police, a lack of confidence in his recall of the events, and high suggestibility.

MacKeith (1992) outlines four factors involved in making a false confession (see Figure 1.1, below) and there is an example of a coercive-internalized situation being produced in a lab experiment (see Key Study 1, next column).

Ofshe (1989) highlights the interview behaviour that can produce this last type of false confession. The interviewer is convinced of the suspect's guilt and keeps mentioning it, along with claims of scientific proof. The interviewer tries to explain why the suspect cannot remember, and induces fear about denying the crime. Additionally, the suspect is isolated from alternative ideas in a lengthy and emotionally intense interview.

Figure 1.1: Why people make false confessions

James MacKeith answers this question by highlighting four factors that all work together to produce the false confession.

- Circumstances – like public outrage about the crime and demands for a swift conviction (as with the Guildford Four and the Birmingham Six).

- Interaction between the police and the suspect – mistakenly informing the suspect of details of the crime by the police which the suspect later repeats. MacKeith suggests that it is better to have a police interviewer who does not know all the details of the crime.

- Health – both psychological and physical health of the suspect. One of the 'Birmingham Six' had stomach ulcers.

- Personality of the suspect – compliance, low intelligence, acquiescence, and 'interrogative suggestibility'.

Source: *All in the Mind*, 1992.

KEY STUDY 1

Researchers: Kassin and Kiechel (1996)

Aim: To create the coercive-internalized situation in an experiment.

Method: Participants were given a reaction time test, but told not to touch the 'ALT' key on the computer. In some cases, there was a witness who made the false claim of seeing the participants touch the 'ALT' key.

Results: On average, 69% of the participants admitted touching the 'ALT' key after this false claim, with 30% admitting so to another person, and 10% picturing themselves doing so.

Conclusions: Participants had 'internalized' the false claims even though they had not touched the 'ALT' key.

Quoted in Feldman, 1998.

Suggestibility

A key to the false confession is suggestibility. In a closed social interaction of the police interview with its expectations and roles, there is a high degree of uncertainty and stress. So it is possible that suspects will respond to direct or indirect suggestions that they committed the crime, and so make a confession. Suspects may be receiving continued negative feedback to their recall, and this can reduce their confidence in the accuracy of their own memories. Accepting a suggestion from the police interviewer receives positive feedback.

There is now a test to measure the level of a suspect's suggestibility – the Gudjonsson Suggestibility Scale (GSS). This involves telling the participants a story, then adding other information later. How much of the later information that is recalled in the original story can be measured, and how much the participant is willing to agree with powerful individuals can also be measured.

Real Life Application 4:
Serial false confessor

Henry Lee Lucas is estimated to have falsely confessed to over 600 murders between 1983 and 1985, and also a number of robberies. Gisli Gudjonsson interviewed Lucas in 1996 while he was on Death Row in Texas for his confession to the 'orange socks murder' in 1979.

There are clear factors that explain the large number of false confessions. Lucas makes the confessions, even to fictitious cases, for the immediate gains (like coffee and cigarettes, to which he is addicted). He has low self-esteem and enjoys the attention, while being eager to please and impress people. He may be suffering from a personality disorder, so that lying to the police is viewed as unimportant. Lucas has no thought of the long-term consequences of the confessions.

In 1998, Lucas was taken off Death Row and given life imprisonment, though there is considerable doubt about his confession to the 'orange socks murder' (the killer was reported by witnesses to be wearing orange socks).

Source: Gudjonsson, 1999.

Summary

- Henry Lee Lucas is an unusual case of an individual who continually confesses to crimes that he did not commit. Gudjonsson believes that Lucas may be mentally ill and so does not think of the long-term consequences of his confessions.

Questions

1 What are the two key personal characteristics of Lucas that influence him to falsely confess?
2 What physiological factors make him vulnerable to false confession in a police interview?
3 What type of false confession does he make?

Differences in suspects

Using the GSS, Gudjonsson (1991) found differences in the mean scores of three groups of suspects: 76 suspects who had confessed then retracted the confession later ('alleged false confessors'), 38 suspects who had confessed, and 15 suspects who had not confessed ('resisters'). The first group had an average score of 12.5 (showing high suggestibility) compared to 10 and 4 for the other groups respectively. The 'false confessors' were also much more compliant. Compliance is the tendency to agree with what is said either to avoid conflict or through the eagerness to please. Some people will make more than one false confession, like Henry Lee Lucas (see RLA 4).

Thus we can list the characteristics of suggestible individuals as acquiescence, anxiousness, fear of negative evaluation, a high expectation of accuracy, and high social desirability needs. The key characteristics of non-suggestible individuals are assertiveness, high intelligence, high self-esteem, and a good memory.

Commentary

Using the GSS, Santtila *et al* (1999) found that alcohol reduced the suggestibility to leading questions, but not to direct pressure. This study, however, was an experiment with volunteer students at a Finnish university.

'Police personality'

There is a lot of interest in whether a certain type of person is attracted to joining the police and the characteristics of that person (the 'police personality'). Skolnick (1975) talks about a 'working personality' (that is, a distinct way of perceiving and responding to the world). Alternatively, it could be that the 'police sub-culture' (sometimes known as 'canteen culture') socializes different individuals into a specific type of personality. In other words, is the 'police personality' born or made? Altogether, however, the police are viewed as a homogeneous group that are different to civilians.

In an early American study, Niederhoffer (1969) highlighted the following characteristics of police officers: emotionally maladjusted, authoritarian, impulsive and risk-takers, rigid, physically aggressive, lacking in self-confidence, and having a preference for being supervised. The problem with such a list, particularly as it is negative, is whether these are traits of the police or labels from society.

Balch (1972) examined whether American police officers were authoritarian, and concluded that they were no different from the average white, middle-class American. In fact, Balch argued against a 'police personality' and explains any authoritarian behaviour as the role demands of the job.

Police officers

neurotic and more extrovert than the local citizens. However, the police officers were found to hold common beliefs about crime and society (see Figure 1.2, below). Meanwhile, Carpenter and Raza (1987) found that American police officers were more psychologically healthy than private security guards, submarine personnel and USA Air Force recruits using the Minnesota Multi-Phasic Personality Inventory (MMPI). In particular, they were less depressed and anxious, and more interested in social contacts. But they were a more homogeneous group than the others.

Figure 1.2: Police beliefs about crime and society

Below are some of the key beliefs of the USA police force that Manning (1971) draws out.

- People cannot be trusted.
- You have to make people respect you.
- Everybody hates a cop.
- The legal system lets us down.
- People need to be controlled.
- Stronger punishment will deter criminals.

Because of the continual confrontation of crime, police officers can become cynical (Niederhoffer, 1970). They come to see deceit, selfishness, cruelty and greed everywhere, even ulterior motives in people doing good. Furthermore, police officers become aware that they can be used – victims are not always what they seem (for example, crimes being reported where none occurred).

While, Crank *et al* (1986), like many recent studies, focused on police chiefs, the researchers found that cynicism increases at the beginning of the police career, then declines with the years of service. There is also a negative correlation between education and cynicism in this American study.

Rubinstein (1973) describes the early experiences of 'rookie cops' in urban America and notes how the police officer soon becomes suspicious of everything (for example, a man sitting alone in the park may be a sex offender waiting to pounce on passing children). This suspicion is not helped by police training, which encourages awareness of everything as potentially criminal (for example, a person who does not 'belong' in certain areas, or an individual sitting in a car who avoids eye contact).

This negative view has been challenged by the more recent research, which has a sounder methodology. Using a wide selection of psychological tests in New York, Fenster *et al* (1977) compared patrol officers with local citizens. The police officers were found to be more intelligent, more masculine, less

KEY STUDY 2

Researcher:	Adlam (1985 – replication of Hanewicz, 1978)
Aim:	To see if British police officers show certain personality types on the Myers Briggs Type Indicator (MBTI) and how it compares to American research.
Method:	The MBTI was given to 304 inspectors, chief inspectors and superintendents at the Police Staff College. In America, Hanewicz had given the MBTI to patrolmen in Michigan and Florida. The MBTI is a personality questionnaire developed from the work of Carl Jung (1879–1961). It assesses the personality along four dimensions, which interact to give one of sixteen personality types. The four dimensions are extraversion-introversion (EI), sensing-intuition (SN), thinking-feeling (TF), and judging-perceiving (JP). The interaction would produce a type like INFP or ESTJ.

Results:	Hanewicz found 20.7% ESTJ and 14.0% ISTJ; Adlam found 37.82% ISTJ and 22.04% ESTJ; both studies found few 'NF' combinations. Both ESTJ and ISTJ types are practical, realistic, organized and good administrators. The only difference is whether they are introvert or extrovert. The 'NF' combinations tend to be imaginative.
Conclusions:	When compared to managers in industry, police are significantly more introvert, sensing and thinking, like routine, are patient with details, and unemotional.

Traditional personality measures

Some research has tried to establish the 'police personality' using traditional personality measures. Gudjonsson and Adlam (1983) used the Eysenck Personality Questionnaire (EPQ) on 112 inspectors, chief inspectors and superintendents. This questionnaire is designed to establish the individual's personality along three dimensions: extrovert–introvert (EI), emotional–stable (NS), and psychotic–stable (P). The police officers tended to be more introverted than the norm (but not significantly so), but lower on P than norm. This is associated with rule obeying and conformity. In a larger study, Adlam (1985) used the MBTI with British police officers (see Key Study 2, page 9).

Adlam (1980 – quoted in Adlam, 1985) used the Rokeach Value Survey (a questionnaire that aims to establish an individual's core values) with 137 inspectors and chief inspectors. 'Honesty' and 'Responsible' were ranked highest of the eighteen values, while 'Intellectual' and 'Imaginative' were placed at the bottom. Generally, this shows less concern for feeling and intuition by the sample.

The alternative viewpoint on the 'police personality' concentrates on the occupational culture of the police – or 'canteen culture' as it is sometimes called – which moulds the views of police officers. Many studies have highlighted how the police label themselves, and stereotype and label others. In particular, there is great pressure to conform to the specific norms of the culture. Even researchers who have been involved in participant observation of the police find this pressure upon them.

Commentary

Practically because of the nature of the job, police officers can become socially isolated (that is, it is difficult to sustain friendships outside the police). Studies have found this to be the case for the majority of officers (for example, two-thirds in a 1962 Royal Commission). Thus the police tend to make friends within their own group and this accounts for the police solidarity. This solidarity is further enhanced by the danger and pressures of the job.

In-depth studies

Cain's (1973) in-depth study of police in Birmingham and Suffolk found officers to be isolated and concerned only with their own group norms. This included the pursuit of criminals by whatever means were necessary (even illegal acts of violence and control). Great store was placed on secrecy and group loyalty.

Smith and Gray (1983) studied the Metropolitan Police and discovered the importance of informal norms more than formal rules (for example, internal informal discipline by peers rather than external sanctions). The distinction was made by patrol officers between 'good' police work (for example, arresting criminals, and excitement) and 'rubbish' police work (for example, domestic disputes, and boring patrols). The researchers noted how the CID officers were concerned with dominance and not losing face. Smith and Gray see this mentality as strongly macho and based around four elements for the officers:

- Alcohol – socialising together and consuming large amounts of alcohol was normal. Not drinking was seen as unprofessional and unmanly.
- Violence – the exercise of violence was synonymous with the exercise of authority.
- Sex – sexist language by the predominantly male officers led to the denigration of women.
- Lack of sympathy for others.

However, Reiner (1985) makes the distinction between four different types of officers: 'the bobby' (ordinary officers), 'the new centurion' ('street-wise crusader against crime'), 'the uniform carrier' ('lazy cynic'), and 'the professional' (ambitious). But Waddington (1999) defends the 'canteen culture' by pointing out that there is a difference between what the police say when together and what they do on the streets. Looking at police behaviour on the streets, research has found that officers are not distinctly cynical nor authoritarian, and are similar to social workers in their attitudes to counter-attacking violence. Waddington emphasizes that the police are a product of the society they serve: 'It is far from the case that the police are a repository for authoritarianism, racism and conservatism within a liberal population brimming over with the milk of human kindness' (pp. 292–3). Waddington argues that the police sub-culture should be seen as a means of coping with a stressful job.

Essay questions

1 What methods are used to measure crime? Discuss which of the methods is more accurate.
2 'There is such a thing as a "police personality"'. Discuss.
3 Why do individuals confess during police questioning? Discuss the reasons for false and true confessions.

2 Criminals

This chapter focuses on criminals – the people who commit the crimes – and tackles three main themes: explanations for criminal behaviour, criminal thinking patterns, and whether criminals have a different view of moral thinking. Real Life Applications that are considered are:

- RLA 5: Smoking in pregnancy and criminal sons
- RLA 6: Born to be bad
- RLA 7: Hostile Attribution Bias
- RLA 8: Somebody's lover, somebody's friend
- RLA 9: Rachel Nickell case

Crime is the product of poverty. Or greed. It is the result of social dislocation, television, the genes or the devil. Choose your decade, and you will find a criminological theory to suit you.

Moir and Jessel, 1995 p. 1.

Psychology is about explaining why people do the things they do. So criminal psychology is about trying to explain why people commit crimes. However, we are immediately faced with two problems. The first is, there are different schools of thought in psychology; the second is, different types of crime have different motivations. For example, the explanation for mugging will be different from the explanation for fraud.

Most of the research interest has focused on aggression and violence, or sexual crimes (varying from rape to sexual offences involving children), or the 'psychopath'/'serial killer'. Concerning the latter category, there are many misconceptions, (most coming from films and TV).

We can divide the many different schools of thought into two main groupings: nature and nurture. The 'nature' approach argues that criminals are different in some way to the rest of the population, and it is this difference (for example, in brain chemistry) that causes their behaviour. Alternatively, the 'nurture' approach suggests that anyone can commit a crime because the cause is environmental or social (for example, the presence of others and pressure to conform).

Biological explanations

This group of theories is on the nature side of the argument and tends to believe in 'born criminals'.

Constitutional theories

An early version of this approach comes from Italy in the form of Lombroso's work of 1876. He argued that the criminal is a separate species, a species that is between modern and primitive humans.

In his book *L'Uomo Delinquente* ('Criminal Man'), Lombroso collected the physical measurements of Italian prisoners and non-criminal military personnel. He argued that the physical shape of the head and face determined the 'born criminal' (or what he called '*homo delinquens*'). These people, he believed, were primitive and could not adapt to modern morality. The underlying basis of the difference was genetic. The atavist (primitive genetic forms) had large jaws, high cheekbones, large ears, extra nipples, toes or fingers, and were insensitive to pain.

The greatest challenge to any theory is the replication or not of the original findings. Goring (1913) compared the physical measurements of 3,000 English convicts and 3,000 non-convicts, and found no support for Lombroso. Both studies, though, had methodological flaws as we would view them today. For example, much of Lombroso's criminal sample included individuals with severe learning difficulties. Furthermore, it ignored the fact that poverty could be the cause of the physical appearance rather than genetics.

One big problem with the hunt for the 'criminal face' is the existence of stereotypes of what a crimi-

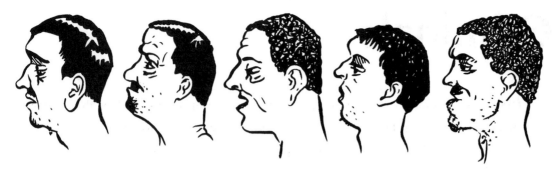

Criminals' faces

nal looks like. The most obvious stereotype is that physical unattractiveness equals criminal, though there may be little evidence for this in real life. However, studies have found disproportionately more facially unattractive individuals among the prison population. But here it could be social expectations that are causing this behaviour. For example, constantly being rejected and stereotyped in a negative way as a child with an unattractive face could cause this individual to become marginalized and turn to crime for acceptance among a delinquent sub-culture.

Commentary

A study that involved giving some offenders in the USA facial cosmetic surgery found that those offenders faired better on release from prison than those who had not had the surgery (Kurtzberg *et al*, 1978).

Physical causes

Interest in finding an obvious physical cause for personality differences continued well into the 20th century. In the 1940s, William Sheldon proposed that the general body shape was the key determinant of personality and behaviour. After collecting over 4,000 photos of male students and 650 possible personality traits, Sheldon delineated three basic body builds (see Figure 2.1, page 14). These were:

- endomorphic (fat and soft) who tend to be sociable and relaxed
- ectomorphic (thin and fragile) who are introverted and restrained
- mesomorphic (muscular and hard) who tend to be aggressive and adventurous.

Based on these body types, Sheldon looked for correlations – including temperament and body type, and delinquency and body type. After eight years of detailed study of male delinquents and students, he concluded that the average delinquent tended to be heavily mesomorphic and rarely ectomorphic (Sheldon *et al*, 1949).

Glueck and Glueck (1950) found that mesomorphs were over-represented in a delinquent population of 500. Thus delinquent males, (because all the work was based on males), were larger and stronger than non-delinquents. More recent research in Britain has concluded that those who commit serious offences are generally smaller in physique and reach puberty later than non-delinquents (Wadsworth, 1979). However, in the longitudinal study of London working-class boys, West and Farrington (1973) found no association between delinquency and body shape or size.

It is probable that linking a limited number of body shapes and sizes to crime is too simplistic. What we can say is that mesomorphy may be related to teenage offences, but not to adult ones (Bartol, 1999).

Once more, with this theory, we have the problem of expectations, and Feldman (1977) notes that certain aspects of physical appearance may attract police attention, and/or influence sentencing decisions. Alternatively, the mesomorph build may be more involved in crime because being muscular is an asset in fights, rather than being skinny.

Commentary

The most recent variation on the constitutional theory of crime has focused on 'minor physical anomalies' (MPAS). These anomalies would be, for example, asymmetrical ears or webbed toes. There is evidence of correlations between MPAS and behaviour problems in children. First, though, this is only a correlation and we cannot talk of causation. Second, many MPAS are caused by physical complications, which may influence the central nervous system, and this is what causes the behaviour problems.

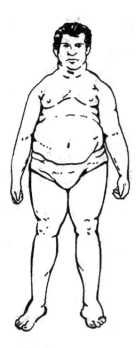 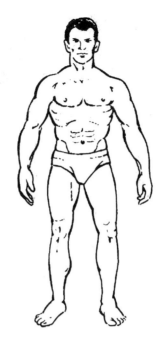 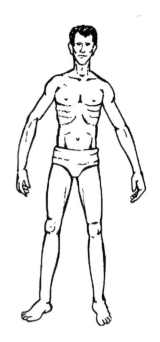

Figure 2.1

Genetic explanation

A general observation is that crime runs in families. If the father, say, ends up in prison, often so does the son. But the problem is whether this occurrence is a product of genetics (that is, the inheritance of criminal behaviour) or the environment (that is, learning from observing other family members). The attempts to establish whether it is genetics or environment has led to the development of specific research methods known as twin studies, adoption studies and family studies.

Twin studies

One type of twin study is known as 'MZ apart'. This is where monozygotic (identical) twins are reared in different environments. MZ twins are genetically the same, so any common behaviour they show, after being reared in separate environments, must be due to their genes, so the argument goes. The studies give a concordance rate, which is the degree of similarity between the twins. So a 100% concordance rate means that the twins are exactly the same in the behaviour being studied.

This concordance rate is then compared to dizygotic (non-identical) twins reared in the same environment ('DZ together'). DZ twins are genetically as similar as any two siblings.

The earliest studies of twins found exceptionally high concordance rates (for example, one study in the 1930s found a 100% concordance rate for criminal behaviour for four pairs of identical twins). But the sample is so small that the results are unreliable.

Since this study, there have been a number of larger studies (but no larger than 50 pairs of identical twins). The average concordance rate for MZ twins is 55% and for DZ twins 17% (Bartol, 1999). Looking at the concordance rates, it suggests that a large part of the cause of criminality could be inherited. But there needs to be caution, as twin studies are a 'quasi-experimental design', which means that they are not as controlled as an experimental design. The first problem is that different studies define 'criminal' in a different way. For example, one study in Norway (Dalgaard and Kringlen, 1976) included traffic violations, military offences and treason during the Second World War as well as breaking the law generally.

Other problems with twin studies include the age at which the twins are separated, how individuals behave towards those who look the same, and even misclassification of twins as MZ or DZ (Shoemaker, 1996). Robert Plomin argues that even identical twins are treated differently by their parent(s), and the twins are only 40% similar due to genes ('*Wot U Lookin' At*', 1993).

Adoption studies

A second method commonly used to study the role of genetics on behaviour is adoption studies. For example, children with criminal parents are adopted by non-criminal individuals. If the child later shows criminal behaviour, then it must be inherited, or so the argument runs.

There are a limited number of studies in this area. One of the earliest comes from Denmark (Schulsinger, 1972) and focuses on psychopathy. The research found that 3.9% of the biological relatives of the 57 adopted adults who showed psychopathy themselves could be classified as psychopathic, compared to 1.4% for a control of non-psychopathic adopted adults. The figures are not very large and are also not statistically significant. Furthermore, this study has been criticized for its 'loose definition' of psychopathy as impulse-ridden behaviour.

Most adoption studies tend to be retrospective and document based. For example, Mednick *et al* (1987) took all the court convictions between 1927 and 1947 in a small European country and found over 14,000 by adoptees. Then they investigated the biological parents of these people for criminal convictions. There was a very strong relationship between persistent offenders, particularly male, and having a biological parent convicted of a crime. But there was no relationship in the types of crime committed, and improvements in social conditions tended to reduce crime (see Table 2.1, below).

Table 2.1: Summary of results from Mednick *et al* (1987) Percentage of sons who have criminal records and involvement in crime of biological/adoptive parents

Biological parents	Adoptive parents	% of sons
No	No	13.5
Yes	No	20.0
No	Yes	14.7
Yes	Yes	24.5

Commentary

However, the general problem with adoption studies is the age of adoption and how much the child has seen of the biological parent(s) (known as the 'contamination effect'). Other problems include the selection of similar adoptee families to the biological ones.

Family studies

The most recent type of research for the influence of genetics is that of family studies. This involves studying 'criminal families' in detail. For example, one study found that 40% of sons of criminal fathers gained criminal convictions themselves compared

to 12% of sons of non-criminal fathers (Osborn and West, 1979).

One important study into families comes from a Dutch family, who approached geneticist Han Brunner. Within the family tree, there was a history of uncontrollable rage and consequent problems. Brunner found a genetic mutation on the X chromosome passed by mothers to sons, and this single change in DNA led to a whole change in the biochemistry of the brain. This, however, is only a case study about one family and caution should always be exercised before generalising the findings.

One of the best, and longest, studies (over 30 years) is by Donald Farrington (1991a). He found that the key predictors for which working-class boys became delinquent in East London were low income, a large family, poor child-rearing techniques and parental criminality.

Immediately what this study highlights is how difficult it is to separate genetics from environmental factors. For some psychologists, it is futile to try to estimate the percentage of importance for each of genetics and environment. In reality, individuals experience the influence both of genetics and the environment in which they live and are reared. For example, in Mednick *et al*'s (1983) study, where both the adopted and biological parents were criminals, one in four children gained criminal convictions themselves. This compared to one in five with non-criminal adopted parents. Genetics has an influence, but genetics and environment together have a greater influence.

Furthermore, the genetic influence can be mediated by the environment. The influence of biological criminal parent(s) on adoptees was greatest for lower social classes and males, and for property offences only (Van Dusen *et al*, 1983).

Walters (1992) performed a meta-analysis of 38 studies of twins, families and adoptions. Meta-analysis is a detailed statistical re-analysis of a large amount of data to establish the patterns of the findings. Walters concluded that there is a significant effect of genetics on crime, but it is small, and the pre-1975 studies have poor methodology and cannot be trusted.

Commentary

There is the big question of what is inherited anyway. There are single gene disorders, like cystic fibrosis, but criminal behaviour is not one of them. There may be up to 100 different genes providing the variability in behaviour (Michael Lyons, *Criminals: Born or Made?*, 1995).

There is no such thing as a 'criminal gene'. All we can say is that particular genes create the likelihood of certain behaviours (Michael Rutter, *Science Now*, 1995).

Chromosomes

Although there is no such thing as a 'criminal gene', for a while in the 1960s, claims were made that criminals were different in terms of their chromosomes. Chromosomes are chains of DNA that contain the hereditary instructions for the production of living cells. In the cells of normal females, there are two X chromosomes as seen under the microscope, and for the male it is XY.

There is a genetic anomaly giving an extra Y chromosome to some men – thus it becomes XYY. It is suggested that this extra Y chromosome accounted for high levels of aggression found among prisoners (Jacobs *et al*, 1965). A number of famous aggressive murderers were found to have this condition – for example, Robert Peter Tait who beat a 77-year-old woman to death in Australia (Fox, 1971).

There is evidence that sufferers of the XYY syndrome are over-represented in the prison population. Jacobs *et al* (1965) found there were 15 sufferers per 1,000 of the prison population compared to 1 in 1,000 in the general population. But this may be due to the low intelligence that goes with the condition rather than excessive aggression. In a massive Danish study, Witkin *et al* (1976) found only 12 cases of XYY syndrome out of over 4,000 men, and none of those 12 were violent criminals.

There have been problems also with the process of identifying the extra chromosomes. For example, Richard Speck, who killed eight nurses in Chicago in 1966, was believed to have the extra Y chromosome, because he appeared unusually tall and had severe acne and scars, which are key symptoms. But it was found in later examinations that this was not the case.

The unusual appearance may, of course, lead to marginalization. But most crimes are committed by 'normal' individuals. A recent variation on this idea is the 'long Y' theory. This is individuals whose Y chromosome appears more elongated through a microscope than the typical one. These individuals were found to be higher on a delinquency scale.

Neurochemical explanation

Though there may not be a 'criminal gene', it is possible that certain genes may influence the brain's chemistry (neurochemicals), and this may account for the criminal behaviour.

The chemistry of the brain is very sensitive, so it can be affected by environmental as well as genetic factors. With the latter, low levels of serotonin have recently been blamed for anti-social behaviour. Serotonin is a key neurochemical, and low levels have been blamed for many things including depression and eating disorders. If there is a link between serotonin and anti-social behaviour, it would be in the area of impulsive behaviour. Serotonin, it is claimed, is linked to control or inhibition of behaviour. So low levels would mean uninhibited (impulsive) behaviour.

Moir and Jessel (1995) quote a number of studies with animals and humans showing a link between low serotonin levels and aggression. Even babies with low levels are more restless, sleep less and cry more.

Commentary

Environment-wise, the brain's chemistry can be influenced by diet (for example, food additives), pollution (for example, lead in the air), or hypoglycaemia (low blood sugar levels associated with forms of diabetes). For example, Dawn Stanton, who is diabetic, attacked her husband with a knife when hypoglycaemic (*Mind Machine*: 'The violent mind', 1989). But not all diabetics without insulin act criminally.

Neurochemical examples

There is also evidence that individuals with low serotonin levels, who do not eat (and therfore their blood glucose levels drop) are more susceptible to impulsive behaviour at that time. One study even found a link between low blood glucose levels and arson (quoted in Moir and Jessel, 1995).

In the USA, David Garabedian, who worked with strong pesticides, attacked and violently killed a local woman where he was working. He was described as a quiet man, who suddenly changed after the influence of the chemicals. The reason put forward was an increase in acytecholine in the hypothalamus (*Mind Machine*: 'The violent mind', 1989).

Whatever the explanation for the change in brain chemistry, it is not a sufficient explanation to account for the diversity of criminal behaviour, nor the various ages of offenders.

Commentary

In the USA, research into biochemical (and genetic) causes of crime is seen as a racial issue. The National Institute of Health (NIH), a government-funded research unit, has been accused of racism in initiating such research. The research focussed on the populations where adult onset of diabetes is high. The main groups in America who suffer from this are African-Americans, Hispanics and Native Americans. Ron Walters believes that looking for biological causes to crime allows politicians to avoid spending money to combat poverty and inner city problems ('*Wot U Lookin' At*', 1993).

Real Life Application 5:

Smoking in pregnancy and criminal sons

New research from the USA has found that pregnant women who smoke more than ten cigarettes a day are more likely to have sons with behaviour problems.

177 boys, who were referred to clinics for conduct disorders, had their records analysed by researchers. It was discovered that 80% of mothers who smoked half a packet a day during pregnancy had sons with conduct disorders.

Conduct disorders in children can become anti-social personality disorders in adults in 1/3 of cases. Anti-social personality disorder sufferers commit 50% of all crimes.

Rather than being causal the mother's smoking may be symptomatic of deeper problems in the family.

Source: adapted from the *Guardian*, 1997.

Summary

• Researchers at the Universities of Chicago and Pittsburgh argue that there is a clear link between mothers smoking during pregnancy and their sons having conduct disorders.

Questions

1 What type of relationship has been found between cigarettes during pregnancy and conduct disorders? Is it causation or only a correlation?
2 How could the mother's smoking influence the unborn child's development?
3 What stressful factors in the household could be causing the conduct disorders rather than the smoking?

Hormones

There are cases of individuals who take large amounts of steroids showing extremely violent behaviour (known as 'roid rage'). Body-builders take steroids to increase muscle growth, but the drugs also increase testosterone levels. Some research links testosterone to aggression levels. Horace Williams (body-builder) beat a man to death while taking 2,000 times the recommended dosage of steroids (*A Mind to Crime*: 'Violent minds', 1996).

More generally, in a review of studies of the correlation between aggression and levels of testosterone among violent prisoners, Archer (1991) said the link was 'inconclusive'. As many studies found positive links as ones finding negative relationships or no links.

Neurophysiology

Post-mortem examinations of violent criminals have looked for some difference in the structure of the brain (neurophysiology) to account for the violent behaviour. Usually there is no difference except for rare cases, such as Charles Whitman, who shot sixteen passers-by from a university tower. He was found to have a large tumour in the amygdala (Mark and Ervin, 1970). This part of the brain is associated with emotions and with aggression in animal studies. However, it is not clear whether the tumour was the cause of the violent behaviour.

In a large-scale study of 2,000 persistent offenders in Canada, it was found that 90% had some minor damage in the frontal or temporal regions of the brain (Yeudall, 1982). In another study involving the analysis of PET scans of the living brains of impulsive killers, damage was found in the prefrontal cortex, which tends to control impulsive behaviour (Raine, 1994). The technique used is one of sustained attention. It involves watching a screen for 32 minutes and responding every time a zero appears. The lack of prefrontal activity can be seen on the PET scan while this task is being performed, plus the fact that impulsive individuals miss many of the zeros.

Commentary

Prefrontal underarousal could equally be found in politicians (Stephen Rose, *A Mind to Crime* Debate, 1996).

A different suggestion

A different suggestion is that criminals have a left hemisphere that is poorer at processing verbal information. In practice, this means that they have less use of a verbal code (or self-talk) and less development of social rules (conscience) (*A Mind to Crime*: 'The Dangerous Few', 1996).

Research with living criminals has found different brainwave patterns among violent criminals. For example, Hare (1970) noted that 14% of aggressive psychopaths showed slow-wave activity in the temporal lobe of the brain (compared to 2% of the general population). This relationship again is only a correlation. So we do not know if the difference in brainwaves causes the aggression or vice versa.

Other research was able to take the EEG reading of 600 children with no delinquency records (both boys and girls) in Sweden. Twelve years later it was found that those with a slow brain wave pattern were more likely to have a police record (Mednick *et al*, 1981).

Recent research from the USA has concentrated on the neurophysiology of children with attention deficit hyperactivity disorder (ADHD). These children are particularly impulsive and hyperactive. ADHD in childhood is often seen as a predictor of adult offending. It is suggested that the frontal cortex is underaroused and is the cause of their impulsive behaviour. The frontal cortex is linked to the control of impulses, and underarousal would mean no restrictions on impulsive behaviour.

Commentary

Controversially, in the USA it has been suggested that this underarousal can be spotted on brain scans, and drugs can be administered even before the child shows anti-social behaviour. The main drug recommended is a stimulant called Ritalin. This stimulates the underactive part of the frontal cortex. It is one thing to give drugs to children who are showing problem behaviour, but it is certainly another to give them before the problem appears. It is assumed that the testing system is foolproof and that our behaviour is physiologically determined. There are many ethical issues involved here.

Other explanations of criminal behaviour

Other explanations have been put forward for criminal behaviour, including undiagnosed dyspraxia (co-ordination-related problems), or undiagnosed dyslexia (reading and spelling difficulties). Because of the rejection caused from having these undiagnosed problems, the individuals turned to disruptive behaviour as a way of finding acceptance (Jane Cooke and Gavin Reid's pioneering study on this was featured in Channel 4's *Dyslexia and Criminals* programme in 1999).

Low intelligence

Studies have tended to find a link between low intelligence and crime. But the nature of the relationship is not a simple one. Rutter and Giller (1983) suggest two possible relationships. The first relationship is that low intelligence leads to educational failure, and consequent low self-esteem. This is manifest in emotional disturbance, conduct disorders and criminal behaviour. The second relationship is that intelligence and conduct disorders have a common starting point, which is not clear at this stage. It may be neurophysiological.

What the more recent studies do tend to find is that the average intelligence of offenders is only slightly below average (for example, an IQ of 92 compared to the norm of 100), rather than exceptionally low. The earlier studies found averages of around 70, for example, but there is doubt over the validity of these studies now.

Commentary

It should also be remembered that there is a question over whether an IQ score is an accurate measure of intelligence. IQ scores are good measures of a limited aspect of intelligence linked to education, argue the critics.

Conclusions on biological explanations

There are many different explanations proposed under this general heading of biological explanations. They have in common the belief that it is something within criminals themselves that makes them different. There is evidence that violent individuals are biologically different to the rest of the population, but it may be the environment that leads to those biological differences – for example, violence experienced leads to 'footprints' (changes) in the brain (possibly short term, possibly long term) (Gail Wasserman, 'Born Bad', 1996).

Commentary

It should be noted that these explanations fit with the views of the time that individuals are responsible for their own behaviour. In other words, the family, poverty or the environment are of limited importance. It is also easier politically to give drugs to solve problem behaviour than to face the fact that it is poverty that causes crime. This is particularly the case in the USA.

Implications of a biological basis to crime

Many people are concerned with the implications of finding a biological basis to crime. This is reminiscent of eugenics, which was popular at the beginning of the 20th century and formed the philosophical basis of Nazi ideas. It suggested that controlling who could have children (and for the Nazis even killing unwanted individuals), would make society a better place. In the first half of the 20th century, in the USA, there were approximately 70,000 sterilizations of mothers with low IQ. By 1931, 27 US states had compulsory sterilization laws for 'feebleminded', insane and habitual criminals (Gibbs, 1995).

Environment/social explanations

Nurture explanations argue that anyone can become a criminal because it is the influence of the environment or social factors that matter.

Learning theories

In the 20th century, ideas of behaviourism were important. Based on the principles of classical and operant conditioning, behaviourists argue that all behaviour is learnt. BF Skinner was a major figure in the behaviourist school, and his contribution was the concept of reinforcement.

Any response by an individual that is reinforced in some way (for example, by money or by attention) will continue in the future, while any response not reinforced or punished will cease. Another way of seeing this would be that any current behaviour has been reinforced in the past. Thus criminal behaviour has been learnt through past reinforcements.

The main general criticism of behaviourism is that it ignores the cognitive processes of the individual, and sees humans as simply the product of past reinforcements and punishments.

The differential association theory, however, is seen as a specific version of behaviourism applied to crime. Sutherland (1939) stated a number of assumptions to show how crime is learnt. Most importantly, learning is through association with other people, and the individual learns the behaviour, attitudes and motives of crime that way. Jeffery (1965) added the concept of past reinforcements and punishments to account for who actually becomes a criminal in this theory. The individual experience of reinforcement and punishment can explain why some individuals from the same background become criminals and others do not.

These ideas so far have concentrated on the past as determining behaviour. But the social learning theory has developed the idea of learning to see it as based upon observing others and copying because of the expectation of rewards for doing so (or not copying because of the expectation of punishment). The individual best known for these ideas is Albert Bandura, who concentrated most on the learning of aggression. The basic design of his lab experiments was to show nursery school children a short video of an adult hitting a plastic inflatable doll ('Bobo doll'). The children then were given the opportunity to play with the 'Bobo doll' alone. Those children who had seen the adult rewarded with praise for the aggression in the video were significantly more likely to copy the aggression than those children who had seen the adult scolded in the video (Bandura, Ross and Ross, 1963).

Social factors

There are a great number of social factors that have been studied. Here are some of the main ones, and their link to criminal behaviour.

Family

The family background is further broken down into size of family, interactions within the family, disruption of the family home and child-rearing strategies, as outlined below.

- Size of family – larger families may mean less attention for the individual child, and/or older siblings to observe as models of behaviour, (known as the 'contagion effect').
- Interactions within the family – studies here found correlations between families of delinquents and difficulties in interactions with the family. This may be seen as constant parental conflict, poor use of language and communication, and mistrust of family members. Patterson (1982) has observed hours of interactions between members of families with anti-social children. He was able to draw out fourteen different things that produce coercive exchanges in these families. One of them was 'nattering' – an extended scolding of the child with no particular focus and no specific threats if the child does not comply.
- Disruption of family home – the traditional view that came from the work of people like John Bowlby (1946) was that a 'broken home' was the cause of delinquency. In a large study in London and the Isle of Wight, Rutter (1971) found that it is the amount of discord and distress that is important, not the 'broken home' itself. This is further supported in that the loss of a parent

through death does not necessarily lead to delinquency.

- Child rearing strategies – in particular, studies have looked at how the child is punished (and rewarded) by the parents for its behaviour. The technique that Hoffman (1984) called 'power assertion' was linked most often to families of delinquents. The 'power assertion' strategy involves physical punishment and criticism with little rewarding or praise. The other two strategies, noted by Hoffman, were 'love withdrawal' (which uses the withholding of affection as punishment), and 'induction' (which tries to explain and reason with the child).

The use of physical punishment has been criticized as encouraging the child to see aggression as right because authority figures use it. More importantly, it is *inconsistent* punishment that has a greater effect in promoting criminal behaviour.

In a large scale study of London boys, Coopersmith (1968) found that inconsistent punishment (often severe) was linked to very low self-esteem and consequent problems for the boys. One aspect often associated with inconsistent punishment is lack of parental supervision.

Harsh physical punishment may appear to control the child in the short term, but has been found to increase the likelihood of violent delinquency in the longer term (Straus, 1991).

Putting the aspect of child-rearing strategies together, Gorman-Smith *et al* (1996) concluded that poor parental monitoring, poor discipline and lack of family cohesion all together linked to violent delinquency, irrelevant of ethnic or social class differences.

Loeber and Dishion (1983) added together family size, quality of parental supervision, parental drinking habits (for example, one parent is alcoholic), and employment history (for example, unemployed father) with male delinquency. So the family can work in a number of ways together to 'create' criminal behaviour.

School and peers

Many offenders have shown low academic achievement at school, but this is not the same as low intelligence. Some may, for example, have average intelligence, but suffer from undiagnosed dyslexia and consequently struggle with school for that reason.

The alternative for the pupil who is doing badly at school is the 'anti-school sub-culture', which may involve truancy and delinquency. Not surprisingly, this sub-culture is based around groups of peers and is not an individual thing.

The peer group becomes important in giving the rejected individual approval. The self-esteem of the individual, in this society, is based around the approval of others and the feeling of being competent at something. The competency may be at fire-starting, for example, but the individual receives approval for that skill and consequently improves his or her otherwise flagging self-esteem.

However, peer group pressure is only one of a number of factors that encourage crime. From the point of view of the school, those with high staff turnover, low staff commitment, 'streaming', and social disadvantage tend to have the highest number of delinquent pupils (Hargreaves, 1980).

Economic factors

The most important link here is between unemployment, poverty and crime. For example, in Farrington and West's (1990) study, the most persistent offenders had worked in stable paid employment least or changed jobs most often. More recently, analysis of data from 42 police forces in the UK showed that high property crime was associated with increasing male unemployment, high growth in the amount of thievable property and high wage inequalities (Witt, Clarke and Fielding, 1999).

Commentary

However, when the crime statistics are analysed, there is no definite relationship between economic factors and crime. For example, the poorest or lowest social class members do not commit all the crimes.

Lone-parent families

Politically, there has been a lot of focus on lone-parent families. Eric Taylor argues that it is the combination of problems that are often associated with lone parents that lead to delinquency, not the lone parenting itself – for example, the trauma of divorce, poverty and mental health problems for the parents. 'If you compare lone with married parents who have the same income, the same socio-economic status, who are living at the same level of social adversity, then there's really no tendency for the children of the lone parents to be more anti-social' ('*Wot U Lookin' At*', 1993 transcript p. 22).

Real Life Application 6:

Born to be bad

Researchers, at the University of Chicago and Stanford University in the USA, are controversially suggesting that there is a link between the introduction of legal abortion in the 1970s and a decline in the crime rate.

The researchers argue 'that when abortion was unavailable the unwanted children of adolescent, poor and minority women often moved into a life of crime as adults'.

'Examining crime rates in the US, they found that states which had high abortion rates after 1973 experienced huge drops in crime in the 1990s, even when other factors such as income and race were taken into account.'

Many other researchers have come out against such findings saying that the link is too simplistic.

Dr Leslie Wolfe, director of the Centre for Women's Policy Studies in Washington DC, says that in fact, since the 70s, there has been an increase in certain kinds of crime, in spite of increased abortions. Look at mass murderers of today. 'They are not being committed by children of low income families of colour, but by privileged white boys.'

Source: adapted from the *Guardian*, 1999.

Summary

• The researchers are arguing that the introduction of legalized abortion in the 1970s in US states has led to a decline in crime in the 1990s.

Questions

1 a What is the underlying assumption of this idea about the link between abortion and crime?
  b Which social class is assumed to be the main committer of crime?
2 What type of research methods were used in this study?
3 How is this view of abortion and crime 'eugenics disguised as scholarship' (Leslie Wolfe)?

Social roles

According to social psychologists, most of our social behaviour is based on social roles. These are parts that we 'play' in society (for example, father, mother, student, lecturer, friend, lover). We 'play' many roles and with each role comes expected behaviour. Some psychologists (for example, Wetherell and Maybin, 1996) have argued that who we are is a product of these social roles rather than any definite core personality.

Sonenstein (1999) reports work in the USA by JH Pleck on traditional male role ideology and problem behaviours. Examples of traditional male role ideology would be agreement with items like 'A guy will lose respect if he talks about his problems' or 'A young man should be physically tough, even if he is not big'. Those teenage males who score higher on a scale to measure traditional masculine role ideology were more likely to be suspended from school, drink, use drugs, or be picked up by the police.

Coward (1987) takes this idea further with an analysis of the male hero in Hollywood 'blockbusters'. She emphasizes that the images used 'present violence as something integral to masculinity' (quoted in Sparks, 1996).

What that means in practice is that much of our behaviour is a product of the situation. It is situationally determined. We behave as the role we are 'playing' expects us to behave.

Commentary

The power of the situation and of role expectations can be seen in the Stanford Prison Simulation (Haney, Banks and Zimbardo, 1973). In this study, ordinary students at Stanford University, California, volunteered to play prisoners or prison officers for fourteen days in a mock jail built in the basement of the psychology department.

Thorough checks beforehand revealed that none of the students who were used had psychological problems. But the study had to end early because the power of the roles had taken over. Ordinary students had become 'sadistic prison officers' or 'depressed prisoners'. 'The extreme pathological reactions which emerged in both groups of subjects testify to the power of the social forces operating' (Haney *et al*, 1973 p 60). This is a stark example, but it is important to emphasize that it is the power of the situation that determined their behaviour.

Control theory

Within sociology, control theory is seen as important. The basic idea is that crime occurs through a lack of social controls to stop it – for example, research found that delinquent behaviours would stop when individuals established social bonds (that is, marriage and employment). In other words, having a stake in society is what matters here.

Commentary: labelling behaviour

Becker (1963) argues that deviancy is a normal part of adolescence, but when it is labelled as criminal it causes the individuals to remain delinquent – otherwise delinquency would be a passing phase. The emphasis for Becker is on the social groups who define what is deviant and what is not. So, for example, a minor theft (primary deviance) is labelled as criminal, and this causes the individuals to continue stealing. Secondary deviance is when the individual comes to accept the label and see themselves as deviant (Lemert, 1972).

The explanation has limited use by itself to account for all criminal behaviour, but may highlight the way individuals from lower social groups are labelled.

Environmental factors

Using FBI statistics, researchers have found patterns in violent crime and the environment. For example, between 1971 and 1980, violent crime was found to be more common at hot times of the year, particularly in the cities (quoted in Sabini, 1995). But this may be due to more people outside in the hot weather than the heat being the cause of the behaviour.

Conclusions on biological/social causes

Tony Black challenges the belief in a 'criminal personality', but argues that what causes crime is an interaction between the individual and the environment. For example, the same individual in one environment will end up as head of a company, while in another environment, he/she may become a criminal (*Mind Matters*, 1993).

Not only are there many different types of crime with different motives for committing them, but no single explanation (be it biological or social) can account for all crime. In reality it is better to talk about multi-causal models or contributing factors working together.

Sapsford (1996) has proposed a model that helps to combine many explanations based on 'domains of analysis'. The *intra-personal domain* is concerned with something within the individual that is causing

the behaviour, like a neurochemical imbalance or a genetic predisposition for violence. Then the *interpersonal domain* concerns the individual's relationships, including in the family, with the *group* or *social domain* linked to how society views crime. Using the domains together, we can propose the model, shown in Figure 2.2 (below), for burglary.

Figure 2.2: Domains of analysis model for burglary

Intra-personal domain	Tendency to take risks because of neurochemical deficiencies
Interpersonal domain	Friends and family who have committed burglary (SLT)
Social domain	Social pressure to have more possessions and the latest fashions as shown through advertising

Another approach would be to look for contributory or precipitating factors, of which the most obvious is alcohol (or drug) consumption. For example, drunk male students gave more electric shocks under social pressure in an experiment than the placebo group (Taylor and Sears, 1988).

In a similar experiment, drunk participants gave the strongest electric shock as retaliation irrelevant of the level of electric shock received. Non-drunk participants noted the discrepancy and reduced their level of electric shocks (Leonard, 1989).

Other theories of criminal behaviour

In the text that follows we will look at the personality theory of Hans Eysenck along with some psychoanalytic explanations.

Personality theory of Hans Eysenck

The basis of Hans Eysenck's theory of personality is the subtle differences in the central and autonomic nervous systems of individuals. The physical differences account for whether an individual can conform to social rules or not. And it is this that determines who commits criminal behaviour. Thus the individuals with nervous systems that are less sensitive and excitable will engage in crime.

Within Eysenck's theory of personality, the most important dimensions are extrovert-introvert and emotional-stable (originally called neurotic-stable) (Eysenck, 1967). Everybody is placed along these two dimensions, and they combine to give four possible types (see Figure 2.3, page 23): stable introverts, stable extroverts, emotional extroverts and emotional introverts.

Figure 2.3: The main dimensions of Eysenck's theory of personality with examples of specific personality traits

Hans Eysenck

Unstable

Introvert	Extrovert
moody	touchy
anxious	restless
unsociable	optimistic
quiet	active
passive	sociable
careful	outgoing
even-tempered	carefree
calm	lively

Stable

Extroverts generally need more excitement and stimulation; they are more likely to be impulsive and thrill-seeking, and thus engage in criminal behaviour.

However, Eysenck had more to say about how criminal behaviour is learnt. The process is not straightforward. Most people learn from past experience (or through classical conditioning in particular) that crime does not pay. But Eysenck believed that extroverts do not condition easily (that is, they do not learn from past experiences). Thus, by their biology extroverts are thrill-seeking, but do not learn to fear punishment or learn from the past. So this is the way the extrovert is more likely to be a criminal.

Eysenck added a third dimension called psychoticism. Putting all the dimensions together, Eysenck predicted that the criminal will be extravert, emotional and a high scorer on psychoticism (Eysenck, 1977).

There is inconsistent support for the extravert as criminal. The relationship between emotionality and criminal behaviour is clearly not supported, but there is support from a limited amount of research for high psychoticism scorers and frequent offending.

Bartol (1999) reviews the evidence thoroughly and argues that despite many problems 'Eysenck's work represents a broad, testable theory of crime that continues to stimulate international research' (p. 77).

Gray (1981) revised Eysenck's theory to focus on anxiety and social withdrawal. Gray's theory has four dimensions to the personality: extravert/introvert and neurotic (anxious)/stable from Eysenck, to which is added impulsive/controlled and sociable/socially withdrawn (see Figure 2.4, page 24). So, for example, the criminal will be high on anxiety and social withdrawal, while the psychopath is high on impulsivity and extroversion, according to Gray.

Overall, the whole explanation for crime is based on a trait theory of personality. However, the idea in which an individual's personality is based around core traits and is relatively fixed over time is not accepted by everyone. A further problem with trying to find a 'criminal personality' type is that there are many different types of offenders. Moffitt (1993) divides young male offenders into four types.

- Stable early-starters (ES) – tend to commit more crimes from a younger age; distinguished by childhood problems and low IQ.
- Adolescent-limited (AL) – less violent than ES; have necessary social skills to survive in later life.
- Adult-starters (AS) – relatively unusual; non-violent offences mainly; no evidence of childhood problems; most crimes among females in Swedish study (Kratzer and Hodgins, 1999).
- Discontinuous offenders (DO) – little research; for example, boys who fight a lot in middle childhood only.

Psychoanalytic explanations

Psychoanalytic ideas come originally from Sigmund Freud (1856–1939), but he did not specifically write about criminal behaviour. August Aichhorn (1925) was the first person to apply psychoanalytic ideas following his work with delinquent children.

Figure 2.4: The main dimensions of Gray's theory of personality

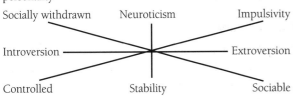

Socially withdrawn Neuroticism   Impulsivity

Introversion ———————————————— Extroversion

Controlled   Stability   Sociable

Criminal behaviour is the result of what he called 'latent delinquency' or 'dissocial behaviour'.

In Freud's theory all children are born with the id dominant. This is the part of the personality concerned with instinctive desires and pleasures. In time the ego develops and comes to dominate the personality. The ego is the socialized part of the personality (that is, it is aware of socially acceptable behaviour). For some individuals, this process does not occur and the process of 'latent delinquency' takes over. Thus the emphasis is placed on the early emotional relationships of the child, usually with the mother.

Alexander and Healy (1935) adapted this idea to see the criminal as unable to progress from the pleasure principle (instant gratification of the id-dominated person) to the reality principle (with the ego dominant). Furthermore, the criminal may be subliminating (that is, acting out) in crime their lack of early emotional ties. Again the emphasis is on the early relationships of the child. In research it was found that delinquents had less stable families than non-delinquents (Healy and Bonner, 1936).

By far the strongest supporter of the link between early relationships and crime was John Bowlby. He argued that juvenile delinquency was an inevitable consequence of the long-term separation of the child from the mother. In his best-known study (Bowlby, 1946) of 44 juvenile thieves and 44 'disturbed adolescents' (that is, non-delinquents), he found that 39% of the former group had experienced complete separation from their mothers for six months or more in the first five years of their lives (compared to 5% of the non-delinquent group).

However, the criticisms of this research are many – for example, unrepresentative samples, poor control group matching and low reliability in interviews with the participants (Feldman, 1977). Further disagreements have revolved around whether the effect of the separation is irreversible, as Bowlby says, or cases where severe deprivation can be overcome and a 'normal' life ensues. For example, in Koluchova's (1976) study 'Czech Twins', a pair of identical twins suffered deprivation in many ways – emotional, physical and social – for the first seven years of their lives, but then after special help were classed as 'normal for their age' by fourteen years old.

Bowlby's study began the 'common sense' view that broken homes lead to delinquency. Clarke and Clarke (1976) have challenged this perception as a 'myth', and longitudinal studies show that the issue is more complex than just one factor causing crime. If maternal deprivation and/or a broken home do cause crime, then they work with many other factors together.

Overall the psychodynamic theories of crime are of limited use, mainly because the concepts are so difficult to test. It is very difficult to prove or disprove that the cause of crime is, say, an unconscious conflict in the individual.

Commentary

What the psychoanalytic view does highlight is the role of childhood trauma, particularly for 'serial killers'. For example, Rosemary and Frederick West, who were

Sigmund Freud

imprisoned for killing at least twelve people, had both suffered severe sexual and emotional abuse as children (Wansell, 1996), while in the USA, Ressler *et al* (1988) interviewed 36 sex murderers, and found that 42% had been sexually abused as children. Hazelwood, Dietz and Warren (1995) found the figure to be 76% of 41 serial rapists they interviewed. But generally only about 10% of victims of abuse become abusers themselves (Carol Sheldrick; *All in the Mind*, 1996).

Variation on the psychoanalytic theme

Another variation on the psychoanalytic theme would be 'over-controlled' individuals. These are individuals who appear to be in control, but show no emotion because it is thought of as a weakness. Then one day they 'snap'. This leads to an extreme outburst of violence.

Special issues

The text that follows examines a number of special issues related to crime – for example, ethnicity, gender, age, whether juvenile delinquents become adult criminals, mental state, pyschopathy and serial killers.

Ethnicity and crime

UK Home Office figures show that more Afro-Caribbean youths are arrested as a percentage of the Afro-Caribbean population compared to white youths (for example, in London in 1984 52% of the arrests for street robbery were of Afro-Caribbeans, while non-whites only make up 14% of the London population). The general perception in Britain is that young Afro-Caribbean men are disproportionately more involved in crime.

Feldman (1993) points out that if there is a generalizable difference, then it is that Afro-Caribbeans commit more single 'casual' (opportunist) offences while whites are 'high-rate offenders'.

There are a number of factors to bear in mind here. First, offenders' colour is only recorded for some types of crime, while 'white collar' crimes are 'white crimes' because non-whites are not usually in the position to commit them.

Research that tries to establish whether Afro-Caribbeans in Britain or African-Americans in USA are more likely to be criminals, or whether their large appearance in the prison population is due to racism, is difficult to verify (Reiner, 1993). If Afro-Caribbeans and African-Americans do commit more crime, then it is because they are more likely to live in poverty, and this is the cause rather than any genetic reason.

Commentary

Almost all of this research is again concentrated on males. Rice (1990) calls this 'machocentric' (male-centred), and it ignores the experiences of black females.

Gender and crime

The most evident indicator of crime is being male, on a ratio of 9:1 (which has remained constant for many decades). In England and Wales in 1993, only 12% of all offences were committed by women. The highest reported type of crime for women was fraud and forgery, but women still only committed around 20% of all those offences (quoted in Giddens, 1997).

Between the 1970s and 1990s in the UK, violent crime among females increased by 216% compared to 37% for males. But in 1993, there were approximately 44,500 violent male offenders convicted against only about 4,000 females ('Lady Be Good', 1995).

The truth is that the vast majority of crime is committed by men – based on official statistics, self-reported data or victimization data. For example, in 1995 surveys in the USA, only 8% of high school females reported carrying a weapon on one or more days during the last month compared to males; 27% a knife or razor; and 12% a gun (Sonenstein, 1999). Thus any general theories of crime must be seen as theories of male crime in reality.

The theories for why men are more criminal vary from genetic on one side to the construction of masculinity on the other. For example, work by Maccoby (1986) has shown that boys and girls are socialized in entirely different ways. Meanwhile Dennis and Erdos have argued that young men, particularly in areas of high unemployment, are in a state of permanent boyhood and never grow up ('*Wot U Lookin' At*', 1993). So a new form of masculine sub-culture has developed in certain deprived areas, of which delinquency is an accepted part.

Because of the rarity of female offending, it has been suggested that there is an underlying physiological cause when it does occur and, in particular, hormonal. For example, in a 1980 study (quoted in Moir and Jessel, 1995) of 50 violent female London prisoners, 44% of their crimes had been committed during paramenstruum (four days before menstruation). This is often called 'pre-menstrual tension' (PMT) or 'pre-menstrual syndrome' (PMS) in everyday language. Such an idea is unpalatable to many writers. But if there is such a thing called PMT or PMS (technically known as LLPDD – late luteal phase dysphoric disorder), then only 3% to 4% of women are affected in such a way as to become violent.

Alternatively, feminist criminologists, such as Heidensohn (1995), have argued that we should look at why females tend to conform rather than why males tend to offend.

Commentary

One interesting area of research is on the 'female psychopath' (who makes up less than one-sixth of all 'psychopaths'). The few early studies in this area find few differences between male and female offenders, except that 'female psychopaths' were seen to have an exceptionally high interest in sexual activity (Robins, 1966). Subsequent research has challenged this idea as a label on women who are different (that is, do not fit the traditional stereotype of female sexuality).

Bartol (1999) concludes that 'research on possible gender differences in psychopathy is complicated by a tendency to equate sexual activity in women with abnormal stimulus-seeking behaviour' (p. 89). When this category of sexual activity is removed, male and female 'psychopaths' show no differences in behaviour.

Age and crime

Statistically delinquency peaks at 16–17 years of age, then declines. However, the vast majority of offences are minor ones. A random sample of around 1,500 13–16-year-old London boys found that 70% had stolen from a shop (quoted in Moir and Jessel, 1995). But because of the media coverage, there is always the perception of juvenile delinquency getting worse and being out of control.

Individuals under 18 years of age rarely commit major crimes like murder. When adolescents do commit crime, many people talk of them being in with the 'wrong crowd' (that is, peer group pressure to do wrong on potentially 'good' people). Peer group pressure is an important cause, but again not by itself. Teenagers who are already unhappy at school may find their esteem boosted by mixing with certain people. But research has shown that, for example, aggressive individuals are rejected by their peers and end up with other aggressive individuals (Pepler and Slaby, 1994). Alternatively, rejected children seek out and associate with other children with similar views on life (Cairns and Cairns, 1991).

There are currently two areas of research interest: first, the existence of specific causes for juvenile delinquency like Attention Deficit Hyperactive Disorder (ADHD) and Conduct Disorder (CD) and, second, whether juvenile delinquency persists in offending as adults.

Concerning the first area, ADHD is a relatively new classification for problem behaviour revolving around three principles: inattention (the inability to concentrate), impulsivity (shown as a lack of self control), and hyperactivity (for example, unable to sit still). In the USA, estimates of the number of children suffering is high (for example, 10 million – Cowley, 1993). It is a controversial phenomenon, which may have physiological causes like an under-aroused frontal cortex, or it may be a socially constructed label for difficult children.

A similar diagnostic category, which is often found with ADHD, is conduct disorders (CD). This includes behaviours like stealing, fire-starting and running away from home as a teenager. It is estimated that 9% of American males under eighteen show this behaviour (Farrington, 1991b).

Commentary

For many parents, the labelling of difficult behaviour as ADHD or CD is a relief because it suggests a medical cause, rather than it being their fault. Among the blames placed on parents as the causes of delinquency are broken homes, lack of attachment and poor disciplinary practices. These factors may be causes but only in combination with many other causes.

Do juvenile delinquents become adult criminals?

The best way to show that it is a number of factors that cause criminal behaviour is to look at how many teenage criminals become adult ones. This is usually done with longitudinal studies over a large period of time (see Key Study 3, below).

KEY STUDY 3

Researchers:	Farrington and West, 1990 (Cambridge study in delinquency development)
Aim:	To see if teenage delinquents become adult offenders.
Method:	411 white working-class boys in Camberwell, South London, who were aged 8–9 years old in 1961/62 were followed for 30 years with regular interviews.

Results:	Of those convicted of an offence between the ages of 10–16, 75% were reconvicted between ages 17–24, and 50% reconvicted between ages 25–32. Those who were the most serious offenders were deviant in a number of ways. For example, at 18 years old, they drank and smoked more, and were involved in more fights.
Conclusions:	The study highlighted the common factors in persistent offending: difficult child at primary school; poorer and larger families; poor housing; and parental neglect. The key indicator was having other criminal members of the family. But low social class, or working mothers, were not found to be factors.

After further analysis of the results, Farrington (1995) highlighted six predictors in childhood of adult criminality: anti-social childhood behaviour, hyperactivity as a child, low intelligence, criminal behaviour in the family poverty, and poor parental child-rearing behaviour. An alternative way to assess the results is to compare the unconvicted at age 32 with the convicted. The latter were viewed as 'social failures' – that is, they had less home ownership, more conflict with their partners, lower pay, and more drinking and smoking.

However, within the whole study it should be noted that just over 20 boys produced half the recorded convictions. So, in fact, it is a small hard core of problems.

A similar study has taken place in Sweden (Dalteg and Levander, 1998). This study followed 75 Advanced Juvenile Delinquents (AJD) at a Swedish borstal in 1975/6, all of whom had conduct disorders, and 68% of whom were diagnosed with Attention Deficit Hyperactivity Disorder (ADHD). The sample, all male, were found after age 28. Comparisons were made of the hyperactive and non-hyperactive individuals in terms of number of crimes and violent crimes committed. The findings are shown in Table 2.2 (next column).

Table 2.2 Summary of results of Dalteg and Levander (1998)

	Mean no. of crimes committed	Mean total crimes of violence
Not hyperactive	3.8	5.5
Hyperactive	10.4	10.1

It is clear that those boys diagnosed as hyperactive (or, more correctly, ADHD), committed an average of twice as many crimes and violent crimes as young adults.

Mental state and crime

There is a small group of offenders who display signs of mental disorder at the time of their crimes. But there are no certain mental disorders that will always cause the individual to offend (like schizophrenia sufferers attacking strangers). The belief that this is so is again due to media coverage. There was some suggestion that Peter Sutcliffe (known as the 'Yorkshire Ripper') was instructed by 'voices' to do what he did (Prins, 1983). Initially, he was convicted of the crime and sent to prison, but then three years later he was transferred to a psychiatric hospital. In reality, schizophrenia sufferers are more of a risk to themselves than others.

Commentary

One disorder that can have some link with crime, though rare, is Multiple Personality Disorder (MPD), known now as Dissociative Identity Disorder. Because of childhood trauma, the individual 'splits' from their main personality. When the alternative personality(ies) take over, the main personality reports periods of 'blackout'. For example, Kenneth Bianchi (known as the 'Hillside Strangler') claimed that an alternative personality of 'Steve Walker' killed twelve women. However, this was not found to be the case with further investigation.

Statistics of crime among the psychiatric population

Statistics do show that crime among the psychiatric population is higher than among the general population. A 1990s study estimated that 31% of prisoners could be diagnosed as having psychiatric problems, compared to 14% of the general population (quoted in Moir and Jessel, 1995). This, though, is probably due to a limited number of individuals committing many crimes, and/or the offenders being more easily caught. 'Mental illness, particularly schizophrenia and depression, are found in criminal populations but the exact nature of the relationship between the two remains unclear' (Hollin, 1989, p. 108).

Meanwhile, Bartol (1999) concludes that 'the research literature fails to support the belief that the severely mentally disturbed, as a group, tend to be killers or unpredictable violent offenders' (p. 143).

A different area of research is with crime and learning difficulties (and, in practice, low intelligence). The early studies found a higher proportion of individuals with learning difficulties convicted of sexual offences (for example, 16% of a sample compared to 3% in the general population – Tutt, 1971). A possible reason for these findings is that a 'lack of social skills may mean that acts intended to be friendly are seen by others as aggressive or hostile, resulting in unfortunate consequences' (Hollin, 1989, p.114). It is important not to fall into the trap of stereotyping people who are different as dangerous. The stigmatization of individuals with both mental illness and learning difficulties is high.

Psychopathy

This category of behaviour, though a mental disorder, is taken separately because of its unique nature. Leaving aside the vast number of films with psychopathic killers, people who suffer from this personality disorder are a challenge to psychology. Technically psychopaths were defined in a number of ways in the 20th century.

The most recent definition by the American Psychiatric Association emphasized 'a pervasive pattern of disregard for, and violation of, the rights of others that begins in childhood or early adolescence and continues into adulthood' (DSM IV, 1994, p. 645).

Robert Hare (1970), who is seen as the foremost researcher in this area, distinguishes between three groups of psychopaths, of which only the first category of 'primary psychopath' is truly psychopathic. 'Secondary psychopaths' commit crimes because of severe emotional problems, while 'dyssocial psychopaths' have learnt violent behaviour from their environment.

The 'primary psychopath', is prone to sudden explosive violence, yet, on the other hand, is outgoing, charming and socially skilled. This person is not the crazed maniac of Hollywood films. Many do not commit crimes, or if they do it is impulsive. The most important characteristic is a lack of concern for the consequences (or others), which means they do what they do without fear (and necessarily forethought). Some would say they are ultimately cynical and manipulative.

Hare (1980) lists the main characteristics as: superficial charm, a grandiose sense of self-worth, a low frustration tolerance, pathological lying and deception, a lack of sincerity, lack of remorse, a lack of empathy, promiscuous sexual relations, impulsivity, and a failure to accept responsibility for one's own actions.

In order to be able to assess who among the criminal population are psychopaths, Hare (1980) developed the Psychopathy Checklist (PCL), which was revised in 1991 (PCL-R). This revised version contains 20 items, and the individual is scored as either 0, 1 or 2 on each item. A score of 30 or more is assessed as a 'primary psychopath' (examples from the PCL-R are contained in Table 2.3, see below).

Table 2.3: Examples of items from Psychopathy Checklist Revised (PCL-R)

- Glibness/superficial charm
- Grandiose sense of self-worth
- Need for stimulation/proneness to boredom
- Pathological lying
- Cunning/manipulative
- Lack of remorse/guilt
- Shallow affect

Source: Shine and Hobson, 1997.

Commentary

Recently, Cooke and Michie (1999) have found a lower prevalence of psychopathy among male Scottish prisoners when compared to North America using the PCL-R.

'Primary psychopaths'

If there is such a person as the 'primary psychopath', then the search is on to find out what makes them so different. A number of physiological differences are currently proposed: abnormal brainwave patterns (Hare, 1970), left hemisphere dysfunction (Nachshon, 1983), or a need for stimulation as the brain is under-aroused (Quay, 1965).

Hare argues that there may also be 'superficial processing' of information by psychopaths. Using the lexical-decision task, which involves recognizing words from nonsense syllables when presented very quickly, non-psychopaths respond differently to the words than the non-words, whereas psychopaths show no difference. It could be that there is a separation of the rational and emotional parts of the brain. Thus psychopaths feel no emotions about the things they do.

It has been suggested that language processing

occurs in both hemispheres in the psychopaths. Normally, language processing is concentrated in the left hemisphere. Using a dichotic listening task, it is possible to detect this difference. This task involves listening to different messages simultaneously played into each ear. Psychopaths tend to do equally well in processing via either ear, whereas non-psychopaths are usually better in one ear (*Mind Machine*: 'The Violent Mind', 1989).

Currently, the most controversial work is attempting to predict adult psychopathy from childhood behaviour. The particular area of focus in children is Attention Deficit Hyperactivity Disorder (ADHD). For example, Robins (1966) found in a 30-year longitudinal study that one-third of the children with hyperactivity were diagnosed as adult psychopaths. The reason proposed for this link is that the causes of ADHD and psychopathy are similar physiological abnormalities (Cantwell, 1975).

It is difficult to establish how common psychopathy is because the definitions of the term vary, and thus so does the diagnosis. In the main, though, it is relatively rare, including among those who commit crimes.

Serial killers

If there is a public fascination with psychopaths, then it is overtaken by that for 'serial killers'. This can be seen by the number of films and documentaries about them (almost all in the USA).

Individuals who are classed as 'serial killers' do not conform to the usual pattern of a murder, which involves a known victim and is a one-off, even impulsive act. The 'serial killer' commits only 1% to 2% of all homicides, but is typically male, plans the killing of a stranger and, in time, develops techniques that go with the killing (for example, torturing the victim before death).

The most difficult challenge is that many of such killers are not clearly mentally ill, and can live apparently 'normal' lives. For example, John Wayne Gacy, who ran a building company, was a respected member of his community. None the less, he killed 29 men and buried them under his house.

Though 'serial killers' are not a new phenomenon nor are they exclusive to one country, it is in the USA that much research and publicity has taken place. At the extreme end, Holmes and DeBurger (1988) estimate that up to 5,000 people per year in the USA are murdered by 'serial killers'. More conservatively, Hickey (1991) places the risk as 0.2 per 100,000 of the population. In the UK there may

have been around 200 victims of 'serial killers' between 1982 and 1991 (Gresswell and Hollin, 1994). In Rostock, Russia, 30 serial killers have been found in the last eight years. This city is now being called the 'serial killer capital of the world' ('The Russian Cracker', 1999).

Holmes and DeBurger (1988) highlight four types of 'serial killers': 'visionary' (responding to voices), 'mission-orientated' (for example, killing prostitutes to make society a better place), 'hedonistic' (seeking pleasure and benefits from killing) and 'power/control orientated' (the sexual component and control being important).

When trying to explain such behaviour, people often assume that 'serial killers' are psychopaths and vice versa. This relationship is unproven. Based on extensive work with 'serial killers' in Russia, Alexander Bukhonovsky has developed a four-stage model to explain serial killing. The first stage is explicitly violent fantasies, then compulsive sadism (often seen towards animals). This is followed by the third stage of physical attack and, finally, serial killing ('The Russian Cracker', 1999).

One model to explain serial killers is known as the California State University Model. It proposes a series of factors which, when they all come together, produce a 'serial killer' (see Figure 2.5, page 30).

There is a difference also with the 'mass killer'. This is someone who kills a large number of people on a single occasion, then usually himself/herself – for example, Michael Ryan, who killed sixteen people in Hungerford, Berkshire in 1984. These

Jeffrey Dahmer

individuals characteristically have no previous history of violence, and this rampage is as if something has 'snapped'. Often they are individuals who have been rejected at school, and as a consequence of the lack of power in their lives, develop an obsession with weapons (Spackman, 1988).

Criminal thinking patterns

One growing area of research is to look at the way criminals think about life (and their behaviour). The question is whether these thinking patterns are different to those of non-criminals.

Figure 2.5: California State University Model

In 'Equinox: To Kill and Kill Again' (1994), the California State University Model is applied to Jeffrey Dahmer, who murdered eighteen men in the USA in the late 1970s and early 1980s.

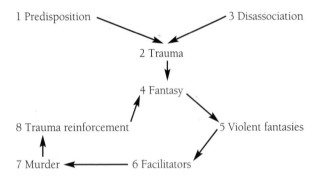

Factor	Example from Jeffrey Dahmer's case
1 For example, head injury when young causing minor brain damage	Unknown
2 For example, early childhood	Divorce; mother's nervous breakdown; father often away
3 Repression of emotional feelings	Rejected at school
4 Comforting fantasies	Examined and played with dead animals
5 Increasingly violent sexual fantasies	Unknown
6 For example, alcohol	Drunk when committed murder
7 Trigger to begin murder	First murder when picked up male hitch-hiker while parents away
8 Murder reinforces trauma and resets cycle; leads to 'rituals' in killing to try and break cycle	Male homosexual pornography and scenes of control

Moral thinking

KEY STUDY 4

Researchers:	Palmer and Hilling (1998)
Aim:	To compare moral reasoning between male delinquents, and male and female non-delinquents.
Method:	126 convicted offenders in Young Offenders Institution, 122 male and 210 female non-offenders. All were from the Midlands, and all were aged 13–22 years old. All participants were given Socio-Moral Reflection Measure-Short Form (SRM-SF), which contains 11 moral dilemma-related questions (for example, not taking things that belong to others and keeping a promise to a friend).
Results:	The delinquent group showed less mature moral reasoning than the non-delinquent group. For the male groups, there was a significant difference on 10 of the 11 questions, and the female non-delinquents on 7 of the questions.
Conclusions:	There are clear differences in moral reasoning between delinquents and non-delinquents.

Moral thinking and moral development (that is, the way right and wrong for that society are learnt) is a product of socialization. It is a product of the child's upbringing and the social values of the time.

Some theories (like Piaget and Kohlberg) see moral development as occurring in stages. Kohlberg is of particular interest because he developed an explanation for offending from his theory. Kohlberg describes six sequential stages (or three levels) of moral development. Based on the responses to a problem like the 'Heinz dilemma' (see Figure 2.6, page 31), Kohlberg ascertained individuals' level of moral development.

Figure 2.6: Heinz Dilemma

A woman is dying from a special kind of cancer and only one drug would save her. The drug is not expensive, but is priced ten times higher than its price to manufacture. Heinz, the woman's husband, cannot get enough money to buy it, and the chemist will not sell it cheaper. Should Heinz steal the drug? Why?

From the analysis of the answers, Kohlberg identified 30 aspects, which were developed into the six stages (see Figure 2.7, below).

Figure 2.7: Kohlberg's stages of moral development

Level 1: Preconventional morality

- Stage 1: punishment and obedience orientation – rules are kept in order to avoid punishment; there is no internalization of moral standards.
- Stage 2: instrumental relativist and naive-hedonistic orientation – the 'right action' is performed to gain rewards for the self; there is consideration of others only when it benefits the self.

Level 2: Conventional morality

- Stage 3: 'good boy/nice girl' orientation – socially acceptable standards important; winning the approval of others dominates moral thinking.
- Stage 4: 'law and order' orientation – respect for authority and the values of society are what matters here; also important is 'doing one's duty'.

Level 3: Post-conventional morality

- Stage 5: social-contract legalistic orientation – the majority opinion of society is important; this stage can be summarized as 'the greatest good for the greatest number'.
- Stage 6: universal principles of convenience – self-chosen ethical guidelines based on equality and respect for all.

Subsequent research suggested that stages 5 and 6 are more hypothetical, and only a few individuals achieve that level of morality. The lower levels are concrete in thinking, and then they become more abstract, based around ideas of 'justice' and 'rights'.

Kohlberg believed that offenders have had a delay in the development of their moral reasoning, so that when there is temptation offered, they cannot resist it. They do not have the appropriate internal moral reasoning to do so.

The experimental research to see if offenders are less developed in their moral reasoning than non-offenders has produced mixed results. Some studies find support (for example, Campagna and Harter, 1975), and others do not (for example, Alterman *et al*, 1978). The main problem, though, is that offending covers a wide variety of offences: offences for financial gain (like theft) or not (like sexual offences). Furthermore, Kohlberg's theory is based on how individuals respond to hypothetical moral dilemmas.

The concept of moral development itself is not without problems. It can include many different facets, like moral reasoning, but also the development of the conscience, and actual pro- and anti-social behaviour. Hollin (1989) also makes the distinction between the content and process of moral reasoning. The content involves beliefs about right and wrong, and the process is how the individual decides what to do. Thus many people know something is wrong, but will still do it. Overall there is no direct link between moral functioning and criminal behaviour.

Commentary

Carroll and Weaver (1986) argue that the likelihood of being caught is more important than morality before a crime is committed.

Links between moral judgements and moral behaviour generally

There has also been some concern about whether there is a link between moral judgements and actual moral behaviour generally. Some studies find a limited correlation between the two. However, in a study of student political activism on an American university campus, Haan *et al* (1968) found that more students at the higher levels of moral development on Kohlberg's stages were arrested for 'sit-ins' about free speech, and anti-war demonstrations. But the relationship was not clear cut.

Commentary

Kohlberg's theory generally has received much research and criticism. One relevant criticism is the male bias (Gilligan, 1982). Most of the early research was with boys or men. Carol Gilligan developed her own theory of moral development for women, which was different to that of Kohlberg's. Generally women are believed to have a greater concern for others.

Development of the conscience

Often when talking about criminal behaviour, people refer to a lack of a conscience, or feeling no remorse for the behaviour. Within psychology, there are two main theories about the development of the conscience: the psychoanalytic theory of Sigmund Freud and the application of classical conditioning.

Sigmund Freud

Sigmund Freud's theory was developed at the beginning of the 20th century and places great emphasis on what happens in the first few years of a child's life. During this time the personality is developing based on the child's experiences. The conscience, for Freud, is part of the personality structure known as the superego. The superego exists in both the conscious and the unconscious mind, and contains the conscience and the ego-ideal (which is how the person should behave ideally). The superego develops at around five to six years of age.

Freud wrote most about boys' experiences here, which he called the Oedipal complex (Freud, 1924). At this age, the child comes to desire the mother, but then fears the father finding out and punishing these desires. To resolve the fear, the child internalizes the punishing parent, and this is the conscience. For boys, Freud said, this would give a strong conscience. The process for girls is less clear in Freud's writings, but is sometimes called the Electra complex. In the main, it involves the same internalization of the punishing parent (the mother this time), but a less strong version.

Commentary

Subsequent research has found that girls, in practice, have a stronger conscience, which is the opposite to Freud's prediction.

Freud and guilt

Freud also wrote about guilt which occurs before the wrongdoing and stops the behaviour. Thus individuals with the most guilt are more moral. Guilt is an energy that builds up based on the child's unexpressed aggression towards the parent(s).

The type of punishment that the parent(s) use is also important. With physical punishment, children can express their hostility to their parent(s) by crying and shouting, and this leads to less guilt (and consequently more wrongdoing). But with psychological punishment (that is, making the child feel bad about his or her wrongdoing), the hostility towards the parent(s) is turned inwards. This becomes guilt, and stops wrongdoing. Thus the best type of punishment for the development of the conscience is psychological, according to Freud.

Evidence to support this claim is limited. One study used is that of MacKinnon (1938). In a complex experiment, individuals had the opportunity to cheat on a test (the answers were in the back of the book they were working from). Those who cheated were found later to be more likely to have been physically punished as children. The participants were all male, and the measurement of punishment was based on their memories. The sample size was also small.

The main problem with Freud's concept of the conscience is that individuals should be consistent in their moral behaviour. But Hartshorne and May (1930) found that the situation is crucial in determining whether individuals cheat or not. In a massive study, around 12,000 eleven- to fourteen-year-olds were given the opportunity to cheat in various situations. Whether they did or not depended on the situation. However, there has been some dispute over the analysis of the results.

Classical conditioning

The alternative explanation for the development of the conscience is that of the application of the principles of classical conditioning. The conscience is seen as a collection of 'conditioned emotional responses'. Based on the original work of Ivan Pavlov (1927), classical conditioning is the association of two experiences together that produces learning. So, for example, being smacked after stealing leads to the learning of anxiety whenever the individual is thinking about stealing. This then stops the individual stealing. In fact, it is most effective if the punishment occurs before the action.

Aronfreed (1963) showed children a toy that they could not play with. It was left in front of them. Half were told off as they approached the toy, and half when they started playing with it. Then the children were left alone in the room with the forbidden toy. The first group resisted longer the temptation to play with the toy. The argument is that the verbal punishment as they approached the toy became associated with the toy to produce anxiety. The anxiety is what makes the conscience. This study is, considered unethical to try and replicate.

Commentary

If classical conditioning is correct, parents should punish their children before they do wrong rather than afterwards. However, classical conditioning ignores the fact that individuals can think about their behaviour and are more than just the products of conditioning. Individuals do many things despite their conscience telling them not to or feeling anxiety about it. In fact, the belief that certain things are wrong can encourage people to try them just to see what happens.

Moral development and committing crimes

Overall, there is no clear difference between those who commit crimes and those who do not in terms of their moral development. Furthermore, lack of punishment by the parent(s), is only one factor of many involved in delinquency.

Social cognition

This term is used to describe how the individual thinks about people and their actions. Ross and Fabiano (1985) distinguish between 'impersonal cognition' (concerned with understanding the physical world), and 'interpersonal cognition' (social cognition). In particular, studies have looked for styles or biases in thinking by criminals. Yochelson and Samenow (1976) claimed to have discovered what these differences are after interviews with male offenders. They found over 40 differences in thinking patterns, including a lack of any perspective of time, irresponsible decision-making, perception of themselves as the victims and super-optimism (that is an, unrealistic belief of invulnerability). But the sample of 240 persistent offenders used by Yochelson and Samenow were judged 'Not guilty by reason of insanity'. There was also no control group of non-offenders by which to make a comparison.

One unconfirmed difference between criminals and non-criminals is a lack of self-control, or impulsivity. There is a lack of a stage between the impulse and the action. Usually in this stage, people think about the consequences of the actions or look for alternative strategies. One suggestion for impulsivity is an overestimation of the length of time intervals and the underestimation of the lapse of short periods of time (Siegman, 1966).

There is believed to be a difference in the locus of control of offenders. Individuals with an internal locus of control (LOC) see behaviour as under their control, while external LOC individuals see themselves controlled by external factors, like luck or authority figures. Again, the evidence is contradictory.

Another aspect of social cognition is the generation of a range of solutions to social problems (known as 'cognitive problem-solving'). Offenders tend to show poorer skills here compared to non-offenders.

Recent research has concentrated on 'cognitive scripts' (Huesmann, 1988). A 'script' is the details of how people should behave in a certain situation and what will happen if they behave that way. These are learnt from the environment in direct experience and from watching others, and from the media. But each 'script' is unique to an individual, yet resistant to change. They become more resistant with use and rehearsal over time. For example, if insulted, a man with an 'aggressive script' will respond violently. He will justify this behaviour by seeing the insult as aggression, and aggression must be faced by aggression. Within the 'script' may be the belief that a man cannot back down without losing face. Thus the 'script' becomes linked to the individual's self image.

Zillmann (1988) sees the importance of physiological arousal with these 'scripts'. During high levels of arousal, people resort to largely unthinking behaviour, and thus well-rehearsed 'scripts' take over. So to teach non-aggressive 'scripts' will reduce violence in situations of high arousal.

Along similar lines, Dodge (1986) has argued that much violence comes from Hostile Attributional Bias. Ambiguous actions, like accidentally standing on a person's foot, are interpreted as threatening and must be countered with action. Furthermore, individuals with this bias see aggression where there is none (see RLA 7, below).

Real Life Application 7:
Hostile Attribution Bias

Bob is a violent offender; he retells the story of his apparent unprovoked attacks, which landed him in jail. But for him the violence was justified because of the hostile attributions he makes of others' 'ordinary actions'.

The first example is a woman on a train who asks Bob to move from a booked seat. 'She was getting rather stuck up about it.' This apparent attitude by the woman is used as justification for Bob's reactions. 'I dragged her out of the chair and gobbed in her face.'

The second case is at a pub: 'My wife's gone up to the bar to get a drink, and a guy's laughing and joking, and he touched my wife up, touched her arse. I wasn't too happy about it, and I told him in not so many words, you know. He stood there and laughed about it.'

After drinking for a while, Bob goes home and gets a shotgun and attempts to kill the man at the bar.

Source: *Horizon*: 'Wot U Lookin' At?', 1993

Summary

- Apparent ordinary or ambiguous behaviour will be interpreted as threatening because of the 'Hostile Attribution Bias'.

Questions

1 What was a contributing factor to Bob returning to the pub with a gun?
2 How does Bob justify his violence on the train?
3 What is an alternative interpretation of the behaviour of the man at the bar to Bob's wife?

Controlling and dominating

Blackman (1998) has taken this idea further to suggest that the persistent offending is an attempt to control and dominate others in a hostile and threatening environment: 'An attempt to maintain status or mastery of a social environment from which they feel alienated' (p. 174).

Commentary

Research into rape and 'date rape' with rapists and male students shows little difference in their attitudes. The only difference is a matter of degree. Kanin (1985 quoted in Sabini, 1995) interviewed around 300 male American undergraduates, of which one-third had admitted 'date rape'.

'Date rape' is the phenomena of forced sexual intercourse after a couple have been on a date together. Both groups admitted attempting to intoxicate the partner with alcohol or falsely professing love in order to manipulate the woman to have sexual intercourse on the date. The 'date rape' was not perceived as an offence when there was a history of intercourse between the couple, or when the man had paid for an expensive outing, or when the woman had agreed to go to the man's house after the date. The same was true if the woman asked the man out, or when she waited until late in the sexual encounter to protest (for example, when they were kissing).

Real Life Application 8:

Somebody's lover, somebody's friend

A new study of over 2,000 people aged 14–21 was reported by the Edinburgh-based Zero Tolerance Charitable Trust, which campaigns against sexual and physical violence against women. It found that one in two young men think raping a woman is acceptable in certain situations. The results are shocking. Researchers found that one in five young men thought forcing their wives to have sex would be acceptable; one in six thought 'if she'd slept with loads of men' was a reason for rape. One in four young men – and one in eight women – thought hitting a woman could be justified if she had 'slept with someone else'; one in six men thought they might force a woman to have sex.

The author of the article, Libby Brooks, concludes: 'It is not alarmist to try to tease out the social truths revealed by such research. It does not demonize men, nor victimize women, to engage with the possibility that men and women see sex and violence from fundamentally different perspectives'.

Source: adapted from the *Guardian*, 1999.

Summary

- This new survey supports research that men may hold similar views about violence towards women, whether they are convicted rapists or not.

Questions

1 What are the figures quoted in RLA 8 if written as percentages?
2 What previous research does this survey support?
3 What type of attribution is made when the victim is blamed for what happens to them?

Attribution of blame

Looking more generally at the attribution processes, Sykes and Matza (1957) have proposed five techniques of neutralization that allow criminals to deny their actions are wrong or harmful.

- Denial of responsibility (for example, blaming their upbringing).
- Denial of injury to victim.
- Denial of victim (that is, victim deserves it).
- Condemnation of condemners (that is, critical of criminal justice system).
- Appeal to higher loyalties (for example, peers).

These processes can be seen at work in a study of hate crimes against the Amish in the USA (see Figure 2.8, below).

Figure 2.8: Hate crimes against the Amish

Byers, Crider and Biggers (1999) interviewed offenders who had committed 'hate crimes' against the Amish community in America. The local term is 'claping', which describes harassment, intimidation, and vandalism. Here are examples from the interviews showing neutralization at work (38 neutralizations in total by eight interviewees).

- Denial of responsibility (10.5% of neutralizations used): 'The harassment was almost common nature' (interviewee 1; p. 82).

- Denial of injury (31.5%): '… no one really ever got hurt, and it wasn't really all that much property damage' (interviewee 2; p. 85).

- Denial of victim (23.7%): 'I always thought they were of lesser intelligence' (interviewee 2; p. 87).

- Condemnation of condemners (15.8%): 'I know almost all the cops … they have probably had their fair share of claping' (interviewee 3; p. 91).

- Higher loyalties (18.4% of neutralizations used): '… it was kind of like male bonding' (interviewee 4; p. 89).

In a study of shoplifters, attributions like 'merchants deserve it' or 'it doesn't harm anyone' are examples of neutralizations at work (Solomon and Ray, 1984). In a study of 100 rapists, most tended to blame the victim (with around 40% even denying the rape) and claimed diminished responsibility – for example, being on drugs (Scully and Marolla, 1984, quoted in Banyard, 1996).

Commentary

Henderson and Hewstone (1984) found that violent offenders took responsibility for their violence only when they felt the victim provoked them. In other words, the victim was to blame for what happened to them. This seems to be a 'defensive attributional mindset' – to blame victims for their misfortunes. The offenders are making an external attribution for their violence. Offenders are also aware of how others will see the offending behaviour (see Figure 2.9, next column).

Figure 2.9: Offenders' awareness of how others see their offending behaviour

Blumenthal *et al* (1999) studied two groups of sexual offenders. One group had offended against children and the other against adults. They were all compared on measures of cognitive distortion relating to sex and rape, and attributions of the cause of crime. The child sexual offenders showed cognitive distortions about sex with children (for example, 'Children enjoy it really'; 'It is a way of adults showing they love the child'), but not about rape. They showed a more enduring distortion overall. The adult sexual offenders made more external attributions (that is, they blamed the victim).

Scully and Marolla (1984) had noticed what they call a 'vocabulary of motive'. The offender anticipating negative reactions to their behaviour attempts to reinterpret the behaviour in socially acceptable ways. So, for example, child sexual offenders justify their lifestyle, while adult sexual offenders justify only the offence.

Gudjonsson (1984) developed the Blame Attribution Inventory, isolating three types of attribution from the answers of the offenders: 'external' attribution by blaming society or the victim for the crime, 'mental element' attribution involving the blame being placed on mental illness, poor self-control or distorted perception, and 'guilt-feeling' attribution, where the offender had feelings of remorse.

The Blame Attribution Inventory was then developed into the Attribution of Blame Scale (ABS) (see Figure 2.10, below).

Figure 2.10: Attribution of Blame Scale

Loza and Clements developed the Attribution of Blame Scale (ABS) to assess the offenders' blaming of the victims, themselves, alcohol or society for their behaviour.

Examples from the ABS

- Victims of crime nearly always deserve what they get.
- When a crime occurs, it is the offender's fault.
- Alcohol is to be blamed for most of the crimes in our society.
- Most crimes can be attributed to problems in the offender's personality.
- If people would stop drinking, the crime rate would be sharply reduced.
- Living in a bad neighbourhood is the cause of most crime.
- Rapists are driven to commit rape by something wrong in their personality.
- Women entice men to rape them.
- A woman hitchhiker is almost asking to be raped.

Source: Di Fazio *et al*, 1997.

Attribution theory looks generally at how individuals make sense of others' and their own behaviour. There are a number of biases at work in the attribution process. The attribution made will be internal/dispositional (something about the person as the cause) or external/situational (something about the environment). These biases are found generally in the everyday social cognition of the general population, and do not make offenders any different. Here are some of the biases research has found.

- Actor–observer effect – the observer will see a behaviour as caused internally while the actor involved makes an external attribution. Saulnier and Perlman (1981) found that offenders blamed the environment for their crimes, while the prison staff made an internal attribution.
- Consequences of action – the more serious the consequences of the action, the greater the responsibility of the actor (that is, dispositional attribution). Walster (1966), in a classic study, invented a story about a car rolling down a hill after being parked. The endings were changed to give different amounts of damage caused. The choices ranged from little or some damage to killing someone. The participants had to say why the car rolled down the hill. In the last group, explanations tended to focus on the driver not applying the handbrake (that is, dispositional attribution).
- 'Just World Hypothesis' – the belief that people receive what they deserve. Lerner and Miller (1978) stated that 'people have a need to believe that their environment is a just and orderly place where people usually get what they deserve'. Another way to look at it is justifying events by finding defects in the victims. In an experiment using a story of rape, Jones and Aronson (1973) varied the victim to be either a virgin or provocatively dressed. With the latter, the rape was not perceived to be so bad by the participants.

Overall, only some offenders show distinct differences in their thinking patterns. Many of the social cognitive biases in thinking are the same in the general population.

Rationality and choice

As mentioned in the section on social cognition, many criminals deny responsibility for their actions, and blame, say, their environment. But how much of criminal behaviour is a rational choice?

Since the 1970s, there has been the development of 'rational choice' models, with the common assumption that most criminal acts are based on a form of means-end deliberation (that is, the criminal act is a means to a particular end or goal). It does not mean that the decisions are rational in an objective sense. In other words, there is a 'reasoning criminal' – a rational decision-maker (Hollin, 1989).

The concept of 'environmental criminology' assumes that criminals choose when to commit a crime based on environmental opportunities and situational constraints. Cohen and Felson (1979) analysed patterns of property crime in the 1960s in America and found they reflected changes in society. For example, the increasing number of married women who worked meant that houses were empty during the day, and thus there was an increase in daytime burglary. Similarly, there has been a lot of interest in 'opportunist crime' – crimes committed without planning. An example of this might be when keys are left in the ignition of a parked car.

An alternative view is known as the 'deterrence hypothesis'. Crime is due to a lack of general deterrence (that is, the threat of punishment) or specific deterrence (that is, the actual punishment of future behaviour). So a calculation is made by the criminal of subjective benefits against the costs of deterrence before a crime is committed. This simple equation is probably more applicable to 'instrumental crimes' (with material benefits, like robbery), than 'expressive crimes' (like sexual offences which seek non-material needs) (Blackburn, 1993).

Thus studies have looked at the perception of risk. In a hypothetical experiment with students, Rettig and Rawson (1963) found that the preference for unethical choices was influenced by many factors, but the severity of the punishment was most important. Meanwhile, other research found that for both offenders and non-offenders monetary gain was much more important than punishment. Only one-third of the participants concentrated on the severity of the penalty.

Commentary

Theories from economics about rationality have been applied with limited success to crime. The expected utility maximization model, for example, assumes that individuals collect all the relevant information beforehand and calculate the objective probabilities of their actions. This is unrealistic. A better approach is to see decisions as based on subjective probabilities (like the available information in the memory). Tversky and Kahneman

(1981) have found that different choices will be made depending on how the problem is 'framed' (or described) (see Figure 2.11, below).

Figure 2.11: Different framing of problems

Research has shown that people respond differently to the same problem depending on how it is framed.

Problem 1

Imagine that there is an outbreak of a rare disease, which is expected to kill 600 people. Two different programmes to combat the disease have been proposed. Assume that the exact scientific estimate of the consequences of the programme are as follows.

- If programme A is adopted, 200 people will be saved.
- If programme B is adopted, there is a one-third probability that 600 people will be saved, and a two-third probability that no people will be saved.

Which programme would you choose?

Using students, Tversky and Kahneman found that 72% chose A and 28% B.

Problem 2

Use the same scenario as Problem 1, but with these options.

- If programme C is adopted, 400 people will die.
- If programme D is adopted, there is a one-third probability that nobody will die, and a two-third probability that 600 people will die.

Which programme would you choose?

Tversky and Kahneman found that 22% choose C and 78% programme D.

If looked at carefully, all the programmes are offering the same outcome, but they are framed (worded) differently, and this influences the decision made.

Source: Tversky and Kahneman, 1981.

Cornish and Clarke (1986) have attempted to integrate the approaches shown on page 36. They assume that offenders have some degree of rationality in their decision-making, but that many individual decisions are crime- or situation-specific. The criminal's decision-making can be seen to 'exhibit a measure of rationality, albeit constrained by limits of time and ability and the availability of relevant information' (p. 1).

Offender profiling

'Offender profiling' is a general term that has no accepted definition and varies in its use between the USA and the UK. It is based on three strands of expertise: statistical analysis of crime data, behavioural science, and detective expertise. Psychological profiling was in fact used in the Second World War to profile enemy leaders to see if they had weaknesses that could be exploited – for example, William Langer's profile of Hitler and his accurate prediction of suicide after defeat (Langer, 1972). The FBI did not take up the idea until the 1970s, but there is now a Behavioural Science Unit within the FBI National Centre. The majority of profiles are related to murder, but profiling can also be used in rape, kidnapping cases, arson, burglary and obscene telephone calls.

The basic assumption is that the offender's behaviour at the crime scene reflects something about them as a person. It leaves a 'psychological fingerprint', particularly where there is a pattern over a number of crimes. For example, tying up a victim suggests a need for control.

The FBI now uses the term 'criminal investigative analysis' (CIA) or 'crime scene analysis'. The aim is to go beyond the facts and develop hypotheses about the offender. The information used includes the analysis of the crime scene, details of the victim and current knowledge about offenders from research.

Homant and Kennedy (1998) see crime-scene profiling as including psychological profiling of offenders, geographical profiling (the area of the crime and where the offender may live) and, in the case of murder, 'equivocal death analysis' (how the murder was committed, and a 'psychological autopsy' of the victim). The overall aim is to look for patterns and to compare them to what is known about certain crimes and criminals.

The FBI specifies certain information before a profile can be made: colour photos of the crime scene, data about the neighbourhood of the crime (for example, the type of housing and average income of residents), the medical examiner's report, a map of the victim's travels prior to death, a complete investigative report of the incident, and background details of the victim. The collection of this information is part of a systematic process following four stages.

- Data assimilation – collection of all available information.
- Crime classification – attempts to classify the crime.
- Crime reconstruction – attempts to reconstruct the crime and generate hypotheses about the behaviours involved.
- Profile generation.

Table 2.4: Differences between organized and disorganized murders

Organized murder scene	Disorganized scene
Planned	Spontaneous
Victim – targetted stranger	Victim – known by offender
Control including restraints, controlled talk	Little control
Aggression before death	Sexual acts before death
Body hidden or moved from crime scene	Body not hidden or left at crime scene
Weapon and evidence absent	Evidence present
Organized murderer	**Disorganized murderer**
More-than-average IQ	Less-than-average IQ
Skilled occupation	Unskilled
Controlled mood	Uncontrolled
Living with partner	Living alone
Mobile – for example, car	Lives near crime
Socially competent	Socially incompetent
Sexually competent	Sexually incompetent
High birth order status	Low birth order status
Father's work stable	Unstable
Inconsistent discipline as child	Harsh discipline as child
Use of alcohol during crime	Alcohol not used during crime
Follows crime on news	Does not follow crime on news
Limited change in behaviour after crime	Major behaviour change after crime

Source: FBI Law Enforcement Bulletin, 1985.

Table 2.5: Comparison of profile of Arthur Shawcross and his actual personality

Main points of profile	Arthur Shawcross
Lone male, 35 years+	44 years old
Menial occupation	Cut food for salads
Appears innocuous	Correct
Functional clothing	Correct
Functional vehicle	Ex-police car
Potential 'police buff'	Hung around 'police bars'
Returns to dead victims	Caught on bridge near eleventh victim
Police record	On parole for earlier child murders

Source: 'Murder in Mind', 1993.

Commentary

There are a number of misconceptions about profiling, usually based on its fictional use and psychodynamic portraits of politicians. Rarely does profiling provide the specific identity of the offender, and this is not its purpose. The aim is to narrow the field of the investigation and suggest the type of person who committed the crime (Douglas *et al*, 1986).

The profile report will try to establish the gender, approximate age, marital status, educational level and details of possible occupation of the offender. There may be suggestions of whether this person has a previous police record and if another offence is likely.

Though there are a lot of similarities in the approaches to 'offender profiling', there are distinct differences between the American and British approaches.

The American approach to offender profiling

The US approach is based on the work of the FBI in response to serial murderers. The main source of their data is interviews with offenders in prison. The obvious characteristics of 'serial killers' are that they tended to be white, unmarried, male, in unskilled occupations, have a history of psychiatric problems and come from dysfunctional family backgrounds.

The FBI tends to divide the crime scene into 'organized' or 'disorganized', and thus the same for offenders. The main characteristics of each group for murder are given in Table 2.4 (previous column).

Ressler *et al* (1986) found evidence from 36 sexual murderers in the FBI archives to support these distinctions. Within the history of FBI profiling, the case of Arthur Shawcross, captured in 1990, is seen as a classic (see Table 2.5, above). Shawcross had murdered eleven women in the Rochester area of New York state. The key part of the profile was the belief that he would return to the dead victims later to re-experience the pleasure of the killing, so the police set up a surveillance of his eleventh victim, and he was caught masturbating on a bridge near the body. To aid profiling and to seek patterns in murders, in 1985 the FBI set up a computer database on murders called VICAP. After any murder in the USA, detectives have to send a detailed report to the FBI headquarters. There the report is compared to information on the database to see if the murder is the work of a serial murderer.

Rossmo (1997) has analysed the process of how serial killers find a victim into two phases. The first phase is the 'victim search method', of which there are four possibilities.

- Hunter – offenders who set out specifically to find a particular type of victim close to their own home. Canter and Larkin (1993) prefer the term 'marauders', and found that 87% of a group of British serial rapists lived within the 'offence circle' (that is, their home was at the centre of their attacks).

- Poacher (or 'commuters') – offenders who set out specifically to find a particular type of victim but away from their homes. The FBI noticed that 51% of a group of American serial rapists lived outside their 'offence circles' (Reboussin *et al*, 1993).
- Troller – this involves an opportunist encounter with a victim while doing something else.
- Trapper – offenders who work in a particular job to allow them the opportunity to encounter victims within their control. For example, Gerald Schaeffer, who may have killed as many as 34 women but was only convicted for two murders, was a police officer.

The second phase is the 'victim attack method', which can be sub-divided into three types.

- Raptor – attacks victim on meeting.
- Stalker – follows victim, then attacks him or her.
- Ambusher – attacks only when victim is in situation controlled by the offender, like the offender's home.

The British approach to offender profiling

This approach developed independently of the police authorities from the separate work of David Canter and Paul Britton. There is some debate about which case was the first in Britain to use profiling.

Many see Paul Britton's help in the 1983 case of

Paul Britton

Table 2.6: Profile drawn up by Canter

Main points of Canter's profile	Characteristics of offender
Lived in area near to area of first crimes (1983)	Lived in area suggested
Probably lives with woman	Recently separated from wife
Aged mid-to late-20s	Aged late 20s
Right-handed	Correct
Semi-skilled or skilled job with weekend work, but relatively isolated work	Travelling carpenter
Knowledge of railways	Worked for British Rail
Previous criminal record for violence (maybe arrested between October 1982 and January 1984)	Raped wife at knife point

Source: Canter, 1994.

Paul Bostock as the first time a psychologist was used to profile the offender. This case involved two separate murders with 'black magic' associations found near the victims. Britton gave a limited profile to the police of a young, isolated man, who had access to knives, with an obsession for 'black magic' (what Britton called a 'belief dysfunction'). The police eventually arrested Bostock, who was a nineteen-year-old loner, a meat factory worker, with a house full of 'black magic' items. He did not confess to the murders, so Britton advised a line of questioning based on Bostock's fantasies, which proved fruitful ('*Murder in Mind*', 1993).

The first well-known case in Britain to involve direct help to the police in profiling came in 1986, when David Canter started to help in the case of the 'Railway Rapist'. This case involved 24 sexual assaults near railways in North London, and three murders (between 1982 and 1986). All the crimes showed signs of having the same offender. The first attacks were rapes, which initially were thought to be the work of two offenders together. Then the pattern became clear, and with the later murders, it was definitely one man. Canter was able to analyse the details and drew up the profile (see Table 2.6, above).

The offender (John Duffy) had been 1,505th on a list of 2,000 suspects before the profile. Canter found that the rapes turned to murder because Duffy was almost recognized by a victim when in court for assaulting his wife. Duffy also learnt police procedures for forensic evidence as he was searched after the rape of his wife, so this encouraged him to burn his dead victims to remove any forensic evidence.

Another famous case in which David Canter's offender profiling was helpful to the police was that of Adrian Babb (see Table 2.7, below).

Table 2.7: The case of Adrian Babb

Between January 1986 and March 1988, seven attacks on elderly women took place in tower blocks in south Birmingham. Women aged in their 70s and 80s, often infirm, were followed into the lifts by a stocky young man who overpowered them and took them to the top floor of the tower block, sometimes carrying them up the last two flights of stairs to the landing near the roof. There he raped them and escaped. Consistent patterns appeared to suggest the work of the same man.

The offender had a limited repertoire of locations, victims and actions, which suggested a man operating in a constrained world. Canter noticed that the tower blocks were like islands surrounded by major dual carriageways.

Victims reported the attacker as black, athletic, without body odours and carrying a sports bag. After the first offence he made no attempt to disguise himself; so he had no fear that he would be recognized locally – the paradox of deep familiarity of tower blocks with the confidence in anonymity.

From the details of the case, Canter drew out his profile with the following main points.

- Not violent because only necessary force used.
- Athletic build suggests solitary sports interest – for example, body-building or swimming.
- Cleanliness and organization suggests he was obsessive.
- No attempts to avoid forensic evidence suggested he was not aware of police procedures, thus not convicted before for this type of crime. Possible previous conviction for minor sexual offences.
- Ease with older women suggests dealing with elderly people in non-offence context.
- Knowledge of tower blocks suggests he lives in one.

Based on this report, a police detective searched through the records of minor sexual offenders, and found a match between Babb's fingerprints and those at the scene of crime. It was the lack of forensic awareness that led to his arrest. Babb was a swimming pool attendant, hence the cleanliness and lack of body odour, and he looked after sessions for the elderly.

Source: Canter, 1994.

Canter (1994) describes his task to pick from the shadows left by the criminals, those consistent patterns in behaviour. What happens during the offence can give clues to the non-offending parts of their lives. There will also be evidence from the interaction between the victim and the offender because we are social beings even in such unusual situations. For example, murderers who kill a stranger without any interaction are likely to live a solitary life (Canter, 1989). Other important factors may be the choice of victim, location, nature of the crime and what is/isn't said, and forensic awareness of the offender, like rapists who force victims to bathe after the attack to remove any evidence of pubic hairs.

One aspect of profiling that is often overlooked is the methodological collection of data and statistical analysis. Often the profiler is no more than a glorified statistician. Canter and Heritage (1990) combed through the victim statements of 66 UK sexual assaults and with sophisticated statistics were able to identify clear patterns in the form of the attack.

It is possible to group how the victim is treated in three ways, each giving a clue to the offender.

- Victim as person – involving conversation during the attack asking whether the woman has a boyfriend, or complimenting her on her appearance. This type of offender believes he is developing some type of relationship with the victim, and mistakenly believes the sexual assault produces intimacy.
- Victim as object – blindfolding and/or gagging the victim, while the offender tends to be disguised. The offender is concerned most with control in the interaction of the rape. The woman is seen as a dangerous object that must be 'trussed and coerced' (Canter, 1994).
- Victim as vehicle – violence (both physical and verbal), which demeans the victim. The actions here are a reflection of the offender's anger.

Canter and Fritzon (1998) have analysed the patterns of 175 arson cases in England and isolated 42 offender variables into four patterns (see Figure 2.12, page 41).

This emphasis on statistical patterns has led to the creation of a database called CATCH'EM (Central Analytical Team Collating Homicide Expertise and Management). The database contains details of over 4,000 child murders, which allows police officers to make statistical predictions about the killer. For example, 62% of killers of females under seventeen are single, but 83% if the victim is male and under sixteen. If the child's body is found without sexual

Figure 2.12: Key characteristics in four types of arson (Canter and Fritzon, 1998)

1 'Expressive object' – this type of arson is the serial targeting of particular types of public building. The offender will have prior arson convictions; he/she remains at or returns to the scene of the crime (this characteristic was found in 46% of the cases).

2 'Expressive person' – here the arson is an attempt to restore emotional equilibrium or reduce distress, and is attention-seeking. This offender deliberately endangers lives, and uses multiple ignition points; he/she usually targets residential property and may even try arson as a form of suicide.

3 'Instrumental person' – the arson stems from a dispute between the offender and the victim (for example, ex-employer); so the target is specific, and the victims known (this was found in 63% of such cases). There may also be threats beforehand.

4 'Instrumental object' – this type of arson tends to be opportunist, maybe by a group together, and could be on uninhabited property.

interference, there is around a 70% likelihood that the killer is the guardian or parent, but when there is sexual interference, this figure drops to 1%–2% ('*Murder in Mind*', 1993).

Davies (1997) summarizes the key clues to the character of a rapist based on 210 cases in the UK. For example, behaviours that indicate prior criminal experience include reference to the police or legal process during rape (which happened in 13% of cases), stealing from the victim as well (40% of cases), and breaking into the victim's home to assault them (in 25% of cases).

Commentary

Canter is critical of media and fictional portrayals of what he does. He emphasizes his scientific basis. Boon and Davies (1992) calls this a 'bottom-up' approach. This is working with the details and building up specific associations between the offences and the offender's characteristics. The USA approach is classed as 'top-down' based on interviews with the known criminals. Canter is also critical of the American approach based on interviews with 'serial killers', who are known to be manipulative.

Evaluation of offender profiling

Whether profiling is effective or not is a key question, and historically there are famous successes and failures. One of the best known failures in America was the case of Albert DeSalvo (known as the 'Boston Strangler'). A profile suggested the offender was a male homosexual school teacher living alone. When arrested, DeSalvo was found to be a heterosexual construction worker living with his family. In the UK, the Rachel Nickell case is seen as a failure of offender profiling (see RLA 9, below).

Real Life Application 9:
Rachel Nickell case

Offender profiling captures the imagination. But with the Rachel Nickell case, its use has been brought into question.

'Rachel Nickell was a young woman who was brutally murdered in mid-morning while walking on Wimbledon Common in south London. As part of the investigation into the killing, a profile was commissioned from a psychologist. A suspect was eventually identified and it was noted that he seemed to fit the profile well. An elaborate operation, drawing partly but not only on the profile, was put together in which a police woman befriended the socially isolated and inadequate suspect, offering the promise of an intimate relationship in exchange for descriptions of his sexual fantasies and a confession that he murdered the woman on the Common. The confession was not forthcoming, but he was still arrested. The case fell apart.'

The profiler must be careful not to believe the myths and fictional portrayals of offender profiling.

Source: Grubin, 1995.

Summary

• The author uses the case of Rachel Nickell to show that offender profiling is far from an exact science. It is important to remember that profilers may be wrong as well as right in the offender profile they produce.

Questions

1 a What is the best-known fictional portrayal of an offender profiler?
  b Is it similar to real-life profilers?
2 In what ways are the British profilers different to American?
3 How might the profiler have drawn up the offender profile in this case?

Commentary

Pinizzotto and Finkel (1990) argue that profiling is most effective in serial sexual offences because of the extensive research base, and least effective for fraud, burglary, robbery, theft and drug-induced crimes. Holmes (1989) feels that it is most useful when there is a psychopathology involved, such as sadistic assault.

Accuracy of profiling experts

In an experimental study by Pinizzotto and Finkel (1990), they tested the accuracy of four trained FBI profiling experts, six police detectives with profile training, six detectives without training, and twelve undergraduates. The trained experts were slightly better at profiling sexual offences in the hypothetical examples used. The experts were able to draw out more information, though, from the crime scene. There were no differences in the thought processes used by all the groups. However, this was an experiment with hypothetical material. In an analysis of FBI 1981 data, Holmes (1989) found that profiling contributed to only 17% of arrests. More recent research has made greater claims (for example, approximately 80% by Canter and Heritage, 1990).

In the UK, a survey of detectives in 48 police forces, who had worked with offender profiling concluded that identification of the offender came in 2.7% of cases and general help in 16% (Copson, 1995) (see Table 2.8, next column). What the survey did find was variety in the individuals who did the profiling. Those involved included clinical psychologists, forensic psychiatrists, academic psychologists, clinical psychiatrists, forensic psychologists and consultant therapists. The skill of the individual profiler determined whether the police officers were satisfied with profiling generally. 'Indeed the research suggests that, at this stage of the development of profiling in Britain, approaches to profiling are so idiosyncratic as to be indivisible from the identity of the profiler' (Copson, 1995, p. 25).

Table 2.8: Identifying offenders

Did the advice given by the profile:	Yes	No
– assist in solving the case	14.1%	78.3%
– open new lines of enquiry	16.3%	82.1%
– add anything to information supplied	53.8%	38.6%
– prove operationally useful?	82.6%	17.4%

How was the advice operationally useful?	%
Led to identification of offender	2.7
Furthered understanding of offender	60.9
Offered structure for interviewing	5.4
Not useful	17.4

Source: Copson, 1995.

Bartol (1999) admits that 'profiling is probably at least 90% an art and speculation and only 10% science' (p. 239).

Essay Questions

1 'Criminals are born not made'. Discuss.
2 Discuss how the thinking patterns of criminals are different to that of non-criminals.
3 Compare and contrast the British and American approaches to offender profiling.

③ Witnesses and victims

This chapter focuses on those individuals who see or experience crime. Often they are the same people. The chapter tackles two main themes: the psychology of testimony and the victims of crime. Real Life Applications that are considered are:

- RLA 10: Source errors
- RLA 11: Victims of memory
- RLA 12: Victims of violence

A key aspect of any investigation and the subsequent court case is the testimony of the witnesses. The section that follows covers the psychology of testimony, looking at, for example, eye-witness memory, stereotypes and assumptions, and emotional events.

Psychology of testimony

Certainly, in court, juries pay a lot of attention to confident and articulate recall of events by the witnesses. This part of the chapter will concentrate on whether the eye witness's memory can be trusted as accurate. This accuracy can be influenced by memory itself, as well as the techniques used by the police to help the recalling of events.

Eye-witness memory

Memory itself is a well researched area in psychology. But one thing is clear from all the work – memory is not a videotape recording of events, and recall is not just about finding the correct place on the tape. Memory includes three processes.

- Acquisition or encoding – this is the event itself and the process of placing it into memory.

- Storage – the linking of the memory to other similar facts and events already there, and keeping the information for later use.

- Retrieval or recall – the process of retelling what happened when required.

At each stage, memory can be influenced by a number of factors that challenge the accuracy of recall (see Table 3.1, next column).

Table 3.1: Factors affecting the three processes of eye-witness memory

Acquisition	Storage	Retrieval
Attention paid generally	Stereotypes/ assumptions	Information after the event
Attention to certain elements	'Efforts after meaning'	Wording of questions at a time of recall

Arousal

Practical factors – for example, lighting, distance from event

Personal motivations/biases – for example, expectations, mental state, prior knowledge, attributions

Acquisition process

The process of putting the information into the memory is influenced most importantly by the attention paid at the time of the event. Information only goes into the memory when attention is paid to it, and only those particular aspects of the event that attention is paid to.

The amount of attention and the process of encoding are affected by the level of arousal – for example, high levels of arousal reduce the efficiency and accuracy of these processes. This is further influenced by practical factors, like the amount of light at the event and the distance from the event.

Attributions

At the point of encoding the information, it is not a question of simply filing away what we saw. All the time we are trying to make sense of the world through the attribution of the causes of behaviour. Thus, we file away our attributions as part of the memory for the event. But attributions are not

43

objective processes and are prone to errors or biases, as points 1, 2, 3 and 4 that follow show.

1 Fundamental attribution error

The attribution of the cause of the behaviour can either be something about the individual (for example, personality; this is known as an *internal* or *dispositional* attribution) or something about the situation (for example, other people; *external* or *situational* attribution). The fundamental attribution error is the tendency to overemphasize the cause as internal (thus making the behaviour of others more predictable), which enhances our sense of control over the environment.

Commentary

The classic experiment is by Jones and Harris (1967). Students were asked in front of an audience to argue against their beliefs on a particular issue. Afterwards, the audience tended to attribute the arguments as part of the speaker's beliefs if the speaker was convincing. Despite knowing that the speaker had been asked to argue that way, a dispositional attribution was made. This is the fundamental attribution error.

2 Hedonic relevance

If an event has personal meaning for us ('hedonic relevance') then there is a tendency to make a dispositional attribution about the cause. For example, if another driver crashes into our new car, it may be attributed that they were driving carelessly or too fast (dispositional attribution) rather than the car was faulty or out of control (situational attribution). However, if it is someone else's new car, we are more willing to attribute the latter explanation.

3 Actor–observer effect

The attribution process is not consistent and we make different attributions for ourselves and for others. The actor–observer effect is where we emphasize an external cause for our behaviour, but see an internal cause for another person doing the same behaviour. For example, if we are caught speeding, we may attribute the cause as being late from earlier traffic jams. But if another person is caught speeding, the attribution could be that they like to drive fast.

West *et al* (1975) set up a situation where American students were asked to help in a burglary by a private investigator or the Inland Revenue Service. The students tended to use the immunity from prosecution offered in some cases (situational attribution) as a reason for agreeing or not agreeing to help.

Meanwhile, the observers to the situation made dispositional attributions, like helpfulness, as to whether the students agreed or not.

4 Self-serving bias

However, the actor–observer effect can change depending on whether the events are positive or negative. If it is a negative event, we make an external attribution for ourselves, but that changes to an internal disposition for positive events. If we catch a criminal whom we are chasing, we may say that we ran fast in order to do that. But if the criminal escapes, it may be because people got in our way.

Storage process

As information is filed away in the memory, it is linked to already existing memories. But it may mean that the new memories are adapted to fit the existing memories.

When we see an event, it is not placed in memory like a photograph. Rather, we attempt to make sense of it as the memory is filed away. Bartlett (1932) called this 'efforts after meaning'. This attempt to make sense of events can lead to assumptions being added, which are later recalled as part of the event.

In a Swedish study, Christianson *et al* (1998) found that police officers had a more accurate recall of a video of a murder than students and teachers. The researchers argue that it is because the police officers have greater experience of such crime, and an improved ability to sort out and analyse the relevant information. In other words, the police officers already have the relevant *schema* to link the events in their memory (schema being currently stored pieces of information).

Stereotypes/assumptions

In one of her many experiments, Elizabeth Loftus (1979) showed how previous associations can become worked into the memory for the event. In a short film, person A is seen talking with person B. Later in the film person A is seen committing a burglary with an unseen accomplice. In recall about the film, participants tended to remember person B as the accomplice because of the previous association.

Retrieval process

The retrieval of the memories at a later date can be influenced by a number of factors.

Information after the event

Real Life Application 10:

Source errors

On 19 April 1995 the bombing of the federal buildings in Oklahoma City killed 168 people. Initial reports suggested that there were two suspects working together. This belief was based on eyewitness testimony of people like Tom Kessinger (a truck rental office mechanic), who said he had seen Timothy McVeigh (later convicted) with another man rent a truck the day before the bombing. Kessinger gave a brief description and police continued to hunt for the second suspect.

Later investigation found that Kessinger was describing Private Todd Bunting from Fort Riley, Kansas, who had nothing to do with the bombing. Bunting had rented a different truck the day before the bombing. Kessinger had confused this observation with the bombing, and when recalling could not distinguish that the memories had different sources. This phenomenon is also known as 'unconscious transference' (Ellis, 1984).

Source: Aronson *et al*, 1999.

Summary

• An innocent man was mistakenly identified as an accomplice to the Oklahoma Bomber. This was because the witness had confused two separate events in his memory as if they were one.

Questions

1 What fact makes the two observations confusing in the witness's memory?
2 What experimental research does this example support?
3 How could the police help Tom Kessinger to distinguish the two memories?

Adding information to memory after the event

Research has shown that information can be added to a particular memory after the event, but that later it is recalled as part of the event itself (see RLA 10).

Elizabeth Loftus showed this phenomena in her 1975 experiment. Some 150 students were shown a three-minute film of a car driving in the countryside followed by an accident. Afterwards, the students were questioned about the film, with half being asked misleading questions – for example, 'How fast was the car travelling when it passed the barn?' (there was no barn in the film). One week later, all the students were questioned again about the film: the group with the misleading questions were more likely to recall a barn in the film (17.3% to 2.7% for the group without the misleading question).

Commentary

Loftus expanded on this first experiment to show how misleading questions and misleading assumptions can influence recall. In a film ending with a collision with a pram pushed by a man, Loftus varied the questions asked. Group 1 were asked straight questions about the film; Group 2 were asked direct questions about non-existent objects (for example, 'Did you see the barn?'), and Group 3 had presuppositions based on non-existent objects (for example, 'Did you see the station wagon in front of the barn?'). Once more there was a memory test one week later.

Group 3 recalled non-existent objects most, followed by Group 2, then Group 1. For example, 12% of Group 3 recalled a barn compared to 8% for Group 2, and 2% of Group 1.

What happens to the original memory?

If memory can be influenced by information added after the event, what happens to the original memory? Loftus prefers the idea that the false information transforms the original memory (the substitution hypothesis). However, there is disagreement over this theory.

Wording of the questions during recall

At the retrieval stage, how the questions about the event are worded can influence the actual recall (see Key Study 5, below).

KEY STUDY 5

Researcher:	Loftus (1975)
Aim:	To show how information after the event can influence recall of the actual event.
Method:	Some 150 students watched a one-minute film about a car going through a 'stop' sign, turning right, then crashing. Afterwards, everybody was asked ten questions about the film, half

---

the students (Group 1), the question was 'How fast was the car travelling through the "stop" sign?', and for the other half (Group 2), 'How fast was the car travelling when it turned right?' One week later there was a memory test about the film. The key question: 'Was there a "stop" sign in the film?'

Results: 53% of Group 1 recalled seeing a 'stop' sign compared to 35% of Group 2.

Conclusion: Misleading questions immediately after the event can influence later recall of the event. Delaying the misleading information to one week later has a even stronger effect on memory.with one question being altered. For

The reason that the question wording can influence memory is that at the time of recall, memories of the event are reconstructed. It is important to emphasize again that memory is not a complete videotape. When information is recalled it is reconstructed from the representations in memory. Leading or misleading questions by lawyers in court or the police interview affect the reconstruction of the memory.

Commentary

Misleading questions do not always influence memory. There are certain situations where memory is unaffected – for example, if:

- participants believe the questioner already knows what actually happened
- questioning follows the original order of events
- misleading information is blatantly misleading
- warnings are given beforehand about misleading information
- participants are given time to read the questions (including the misleading ones) carefully.

Other issues with eye-witness memory

These include the three issues that follow.

1 Confidence of the witness
The confidence of the accuracy of recall by the witness does not equal actual accuracy of recall. When

working with police officers, Clark and Stephenson (1995) asked them to recall an event when they were working alone, or as a pair, or as a group of four. In free and cued recall, all the conditions were equally accurate, with the group of four remembering most information. But the group of four were confident of their accuracy when they were right and also when wrong. Thus the joint testimony of four people was more accurate and produced more information, but when they were wrong, they were still wrong.

2 Estimations
Buckhout (1974) staged a 'crime' in a lecture theatre in front of 141 students. All were interviewed about what had happened. The students tended to overestimate the length of time of the incident (that is, twice as long as it actually was). There was a 25% accuracy in the description of the suspect, while 40% of the students correctly identified the suspect from six photographs presented. However, 25% identified an innocent bystander as the suspect from the six photographs.

3 Emotional events
On the whole, strong negative emotions reduce the accuracy of recall of an event. Loftus *et al* (1983) showed participants a stressful film of a hospital fire. Later recall was impaired by reminding participants of the fire. Hollin (1989) has noted that violence decreases the accuracy of the recall.

However, Malpass and Devine (1981) found different results. Recall was increased for a staged act of vandalism by reminding participants of the main events and exploring their feelings at the time. The difference in results between the studies may be due to the difference in events used, whether it is a lab experiment or a real life study, or whether the individual is directly affected. For example, actually experiencing violence has a different effect to watching a film.

Loftus *et al* (1987) have highlighted what is called the 'weapon focus effect'. This is the tendency of the witness to focus on the weapon of the offender at the expense of details of the face, for example.

Commentary

Mitchell *et al* (1998) have challenged this attentional problem for weapons, by showing the same effect if the offender is carrying a piece of celery. It is the novelty of the event that influences recall in the eye witness situation.

Conclusions

We can conclude from the above studies that eye-witness memory is far from perfect and needs to be used with caution. Buckhout (1974) emphasizes that 'Perception and memory are decision-making processes affected by the totality of a person's abilities, background, attitudes, motives and beliefs, by environment and by the way his recollection is eventually tested'.

However, not all memories are distorted. Loftus (1979) showed a film about a red purse being stolen from a handbag. After the film, viewers were asked if they saw the brown purse being stolen. One week later, only 2% of these recalled a brown purse in the film. The memory for major facts is not easily misled. There are key aspects to the influence of misleading information after the event: it only influences memory if it is about minor details of the event, it is given after a delay, and the witness is not aware that false information is being given.

Commentary

Almost all of the research is lab-based experimental work, usually with students watching a short film followed by questions. Certainly, the work of Elizabeth Loftus is like that. This type of research tends to paint a very negative picture of eye-witness accuracy. But is this the same as real-life witnesses?

Real-life studies

There are a limited number of real-life studies to challenge the conclusions of the lab experiments, and they suggest that eye-witness memory is more accurate than first thought.

In particular, in a Canadian study by Yuille and Cutshall (1986), the researchers made use of a local shooting and robbery in Vancouver, and found that the accuracy of recall did not decline even after five months. The shooting took place outside a gun shop in view of several witnesses, and involved the thief firing two shots and the shop-owner six. Thirteen of the twenty-one witnesses were traced five months after the event by the researchers. The level of accuracy was 'truly impressive' when compared to the original police reports. Misleading questions had no effect on accuracy of recall. Any errors in information were due to the position of the witness rather than recall of false information (confabulations). Those deeply affected by the event were most accurate. So when an event is personally meaningful, rather than being an experimental video, then eye-witness memory is good.

Methods used by the police to help in recall

There are several of these including identity parades, using photographs, photo-fit systems and drug-aided interviews. Each of these is examined in the text that follows.

Identity parades

A common practice by the police is to place a suspect in an identity parade with five or six other people. The witness then has to pick out the suspect. Walking down the line of people and pointing out the suspect can often make the witness nervous, which thereby reduces recall. But use of a one-way mirror (where the witness can see the suspects, but they can't see the witness) increases the accuracy of recall in identity parades.

The problem generally with identity parades is that the police tend to choose people who look roughly similar. This is a legal requirement to avoid suggestion, but it tends to make accurate recall more difficult. The identity parade cannot be completely free of suggestion because the witness is under pressure to choose someone. The identity parade only takes place because the police have a suspect. Buckhout (1974) found in his experiments that rarely do witnesses say 'I don't know'. 'The social influence of the line-up itself seems to encourage a "yes" response.'

Commentary

Stephenson (1992) has looked at how unconscious influences can be placed on the witness during the identity parade through – for example, the position of the suspect in the parade or the non-verbal behaviour of the police officers. In a mock identity parade, Stephenson used experimenters who either knew who was the correct suspect or not. In the former condition, there were significantly more correct choices by the participants than in the latter.

Avoiding bias in identity parades

One way to avoid bias in identity parades is to tell the witness beforehand that the suspect may or may not be in the parade, and then to not always include the suspect in the identity parade.

'Mugshots' (books of photographs of suspects)

Another popular method for the police to help recall is to get the witness to look through photographs of known criminals to find the suspect.

Wells et al (1979) set up an experiment where participants saw a calculator taken from a room where they were waiting. Afterwards 58% of the participants correctly identified the suspect from a choice of six photographs. However, Buckhout (1974) argues that participants will pick out the unusual photograph from a group of photographs, even though 75% of participants had not seen the person before.

Recognition of faces is poor if the face changes between the encoding and the presentation of possibilities. This could be a change in glasses, hairstyle, beard or even expression. Patterson and Baddeley (1977) compared the accuracy of recall of a face that had changed in some way between the first and second time the participants saw it. For example, a change of wig reduces the accuracy of recall to 50%, while a change of wig and beard leads to only 30% accurate recall. These figures compare to 70% accuracy when the face does not change.

The accuracy of face recall is also influenced by: length of time since the face was seen, the seriousness of crime, the number of previous encounters with the suspect, and witness characteristics (like attention to detail).

Commentary

The most confusing method for recall is to show 'mugshots', then have an identity parade. This leads to confusion between recognition and episodic memory. In other words, the witness may recognize a face in the identity parade, but not know if it comes from the original event or from the 'mugshots'.

Photo-fit systems

Traditionally this could mean a police artist or a series of cards with parts of the face being combined to give the 'photo-fit'. This latter practice is very restrictive, and assumes that individual features can be discriminated and combined to make the face.

Recent research suggests the whole face is recalled. Thus computer-based photo-fits, like 'E-Fit' or 'CompuFit', are based around the whole face. Early research finds these systems no better than traditional methods in accuracy of recall of faces, however (Graham Davies, 1996, speaking on *Science Now*). It is important that any system used to help recall of faces is based on the psychological research of how we recognize familiar faces.

Commentary: Face recognition for familiar faces

The recognition of familiar faces and the naming of the person can be seen to have three stages.

- The face is compared with a set of stored descriptions

called 'face recognition units' (FRU), and this produces a feeling of familiarity or not.

- The memory store is activated to recall facts about the person.
- The retrieval of the name of the person is then made.

The research has tended to concentrate on whether the stored descriptions are based on individual features or the whole face. One possibility is a representation of how each face differs from the average prototype, and thus distinctiveness is the key (Bruce 1988).

Using computer images, Haigh (1986) found that the shape of the head was most important, followed by the eyes and mouth in full-face recognition, while the nose is more important in profile recognition.

Forensic hypnosis

In America, forensic or investigative hypnosis has been used to attempt to gain more recall of information. Forensic hypnosis is a specific use of the technique of hypnosis: 'information-gathering for evidential purposes'. It is believed that under hypnosis, the witness will be able to access consciously forgotten information. This is sometimes called 'hypnotic hypermnesia'.

Though it is still used, the research tends to paint a negative picture of its effectiveness. The main feeling is that during hypnosis witnesses are relaxed and, in fact, very suggestible. Thus they are easily misled by the interviewer.

Orne (1979) quotes the case of an FBI suspect who described details of an event while hypnotized. Later it was found that this suspect had been out of the country at the time of the crime and could not have witnessed what he described under hypnosis.

Sanders and Simmons (1983) set up a lab experiment with a video of a pick-pocket, then an interview about the film and an identity parade. Half of the participants were hypnotized, the other half not, for the interview and identity parade. The hypnotized participants were: less accurate in the identification of the suspect, less accurate in answers to questions, equally confident when right or wrong about their recall, and easily misled in the identity parade (for example, by another person wearing the same clothes as the suspect in the video).

Geiselman and Machlowitz (1987) reviewed 38 studies comparing hypnosis with an ordinary police interview in terms of correct recall and errors. Twenty-one studies showed significantly more correct information recalled with hypnosis, thirteen studies showed no difference, and the other four had significantly less information under hypnosis. But eight of the studies showed a significant increase in errors with hypnosis, while ten studies showed no effect.

Commentary: Drug-aided interviews

Drug-aided interviews involve the use of drugs, such as sodium amytal, which reduces inhibitions and encourages the person to talk. Any evidence gained with this method is not acceptable in court in most countries. The main reason is the serious problem of the reliability of the information obtained during the procedure (that is, the inclusion of fantasy).

Best methods for remembering events

The best methods for remembering events include reliving the event, following the order of events and cognitive interviews. Each of these is explained in the text that follows.

Reliving the event

This involves taking the witness through the event and reliving it where it happened – that is, returning to the scene of the crime. The assumption is that as we are encoding information about the event, we also encode information about the environment. Being in the environment again acts as a cue to recall more information about the event. Tulving and Thomson (1973) called this the Encoding Specificity Principle. Cues incorporated at encoding can be used to help retrieval.

Commentary

A number of computer graphic techniques are being tried by the UK police. One of them is CAMERA (Computer Aided Manoeuvre Evaluation Reconstruction and Analysis). It builds up a picture of the event from the witness's point of view using scenarios from its memory (Roy 1991). This can be used where returning to the scene of the crime is not possible or feasible.

Following the order of events

Questioning produces much better recall if it follows the chronological order of the events rather than asking questions in any order. Using a video of a car chase after a crime, Morris and Morris (1985) tested this principle in a lab experiment. Participants were asked 23 questions after the film: for half of them the order of the questions followed the time sequence of the film, while for the other half the questions were random. The first group produced 20% better recall.

Cognitive interviews

In recent years, psychologists working with the police in America and the UK have concentrated on the police interview with the witness. Traditionally, there has been little training and police officers ask whatever questions they feel are relevant, frequently interrupt, ask short-answer questions, and follow inappropriate sequences of questioning (Fisher *et al*, 1987). They also tend to ignore apparently irrelevant material. Fisher *et al*, when working with the Florida Police Department, analysed the traditional police interview. Interruptions would occur as early as seven seconds into the witness's narrative and few witnesses were allowed to finish their narratives. In the interviews, there was an average of 26 short-answer questions and three open-ended questions.

The view now is that there is always more information in the witness's memory than initially recalled. The cognitive interview (CI) was developed from the research of memory and aims to help the witness find cues that lead to recall of the event. The CI has 4 stages, which need to be followed in order.

1 Witnesses are asked to reinstate their feelings and the context of the event. They may be encouraged to close their eyes and concentrate. When people are asked to recall classmates at school, they report picturing the classroom and moving around it in their mind. This has highlighted the importance of reinstating the context.
2 The witness is asked to tell the story of what happened, without interruptions, leaving no details out, even apparently irrelevant ones. It is believed that apparently irrelevant information may act as a trigger for relevant information.
3 Then the witness recalls the event in a different order, such as backwards, again looking for cues to trigger more memories.
4 The witness finally recounts what happened from the point of view of another witness. Some of this information may be speculation, but again cues may trigger memories.

These principles of the CI can be easily taught to interviewers of witnesses of crimes, of child abuse victims, and of accident survivors. In fact, in America after one hour's training in the use of the CI, sixth-formers were able to find more details than experienced police officers using the standard interview (Graham Davies speaking on *Science Now*, 1991).

Geiselman *et al* (1985) produced one of the first evaluation studies for the CI. They compared the CI with the standard interview (SI) and hypnosis using the Los Angeles Police Department. The researchers used a film, then 48 hours later an interview about it. Performance was measured by the number of facts accurately recalled and the number of errors in recall (see Table 3.2, below).

Table 3.2: Summary of results of Geiselman *et al* (1985)

	SI	CI	Hypnosis
Number of items accurately recalled	29.0	41.2	38.0
Mean number of errors	6.1	7.3	5.9

Thus, the CI produced more information than the other methods with only a slight increase in the number of recall errors.

Kohnken (1996) more recently performed a meta-analysis on 41 lab experiments, with over 1,500 participants in total, comparing the CI and the standard interview. The CI produced around 40% more accurate information and both techniques had 15% of errors in recall. But these were all lab experiments.

Commentary: Cognitive interviews with children

In recent years, attempts have been made to extend the CI for use with children. Memon *et al* (1997) showed 87 8–9 year olds a magic show followed, at a later date, by a standard interview about what they remembered, or a specially adapted CI for children. Used after two days, the CI produced more information than the standard interview, both correct and erroneus. After twelve days, there was no difference between the two techniques.

Hayes and Delamothe (1997) used groups of 5–7 and 9–11 year olds in a similar experiment. They found that the CI produced more accurate recall for both age groups, but there was no difference in susceptibility to misleading questions with the CI or the standard interview. In practice, the CI is not always used with children, particularly younger than seven years old.

Evaluation of the cognitive interview

Generally, the CI appears to be successful for adults, but it is not without its critics. In particular, the use of 'visualization' (closing the eyes and imagining being back at the scene of the event) could be taken as a mild form of hypnosis. But Graham Davies (speaking on *Science Now*, 1991) argues that there is no altered state of awareness (as with hypnosis), and thus the CI is less open to suggestibility.

Asking the witnesses to describe what other witnesses might have seen is usually guessing, and these may become confused with the facts. The problem remains how to increase recall without increasing the number of errors.

Mistaken identity

Real Life Application 11:

Victims of memory

Nancy Stone was a rape victim who picked her attacker from an identity parade and confidently pointed him out in court. But the person she chose, Steve Titus, was wrongly convicted – as later evidence showed. Nancy Stone was not lying, but was mistaken. How could this happen?

Elizabeth Loftus highlights three post-processes that can explain such a mistaken identity

- 'Weapon focus' – the victim focused on the knife and did not really look at her attacker.
- 'Suggestive questioning' – the victim was shown 'mugshots' then an identity parade. There is an implicit pressure to choose someone from the identity parade.
- 'Photo-bias effect' – Loftus' research has shown that false choices will be made in the identity parade 20% of the time, simply because the victim has been seen in the 'mugshot' earlier. This compares with 8% if there is just an identity parade.

It was only when a rapist was later arrested that he confessed to Nancy Stone's attack. Steve Titus was released, his life completely changed, and he died soon after from a heart attack.

Source: adapted from *Discover Magazine*, 1999.

Summary

- Witnesses can identify the wrong suspect not because they are lying but because they are mistaken.

Questions

1 What stage in the three processes of memory would the attention to the weapon influence most?
2 Why does showing witnesses 'mugshots' before an identity parade reduce their accuracy of recall?
3 What other examples of implicit pressure to choose someone from an identity parade can you think of?

Isolating mistaken identity into two groups of variables

So far we have emphasised how eye-witness memory is far from perfect. But this is still different to mistaken identity leading to a false conviction. Rattner (1988) looked at a number of miscarriages of justice, and found that in half of the cases, the witness making the wrong identification was to blame. This is not necessarily because the witness is lying, they genuinely believe in their identification. But it is because they are mistaken (see RLA 11, page 50).

Mistaken identity can be isolated to two groups of variables: *estimator* variables and *system* variables (Wells, 1978).

1 Estimator variables

These are aspects of the witness, the target and the witnessed event that reduce the accuracy of memory.

Shapiro and Penrod (1996) performed a meta-analysis on 128 experiments with 960 conditions, over 17,000 participants and more than 700,000 separate recognition judgements. They were able to draw out the following important variables.

- Stable characteristics of the eye witness – personality has no relationship to accuracy of recall, though children and older adults are poorer on recognition than adults generally. O'Rourke *et al* (1989) compared the accuracy of identification of robbers by different age groups: 20 year olds had an average of 50% correct identification, while for 60 year olds, it was only 25%.
- Malleable characteristics of the eye-witness – training or expectation of later testing does not improve accuracy. The key is deeper processing of the information (that is, linking to other information in memory).
- Additional eye-witness testimony factors – confidence of the witness or consistency between multiple descriptions of the same event are not reliable predictors of actual accuracy. But other research suggests that confidence of accuracy is a better indicator of accuracy for 'choosers' (that is, witnesses who identify a person) than 'non-choosers'.
- Stable target characteristics – highly physically attractive or unattractive faces are better recognized than the average.
- Malleable target characteristics – disguises in any form reduce accuracy of identification.
- Environmental conditions – the length of exposure to the event, the presence or absence of a weapon, whether the witness was intoxicated, and the level of stress will all influence identification.
- Post-event factors – for example, the time between the crime and recall.

2 System variables

These are variables in the identification process that can lead to mistaken identification.

- Random error – this is the chance misidentification because, for example, the witness believes he/she already knows the criminal.
- Systematic error – there are two types: structural and procedural error. Structural error is concerned with bias in the identification procedure (for example, composition of the identity parade or the arrangement of photographs leading to bias). In a lab experiment, individuals who are noticeably different in line-ups are incorrectly identified as the suspect by 70% of the participants (Lindsey and Wells, 1980). Procedural error can be due to errors during the recognition testing (for example, 'mugshots' followed by an identity parade, or police officers may give non-verbal cues as to who they think the suspect is in the choice of photographs shown to the witness).

Commentary

Research shows that asking 'Are you sure?' when what the police think is the wrong photograph is chosen tends to cause the witness to doubt. Alternatively, a simple smile by the officer at the right photograph being viewed encourages the choice of that photograph.

Conclusion on mistaken identity

Identification or mistaken identification of the suspect is not only influenced by the witness's memory and those limitations, the suspect themselves and the environment, but also by the process of recall. On that basis, it is quite easy to see how eye witnesses make mistaken identifications.

Victims

The next section of this chapter looks at who the victims are, fear of crime, effects of victimization, victim-offender interaction and help available to victims.

Who is the victim?

The traditional ways of collecting crime figures from police records often ignore the victim. So it is better to use victim surveys. Victim surveys give details of the extent of crime and also the effects of it. Victim surveys are relatively new – the first national one in the USA was in 1972, and in Britain 1983.

A good survey will aim for a cross-section of the population to sample. The British Crime Survey in 1988 (Mayhew *et al*, 1989) set the pattern by sampling nearly 14,000 addresses based on parliamentary constituencies and a sample of adults from each household. Each of the individuals sampled filled in four questionnaires.

It is important to note that not all crimes are reported by the victims. The most obvious case is when both the offender and the victim are breaking the law. The British Crime Surveys show a number of reasons why certain crimes remain unreported by the victims (see Table 3.3, below).

Table 3.3: Main reasons given by victims for not reporting crime to police

Reason	Example
Too trivial; no loss	Theft from motor vehicle
Police could do nothing, police not interested, police not trusted, inconvenient to report	Robbery
Dealt with matter ourselves	Theft in a dwelling – for example, legitimate visitor to house steals something
Reported to other authorities	Personal theft – for example, theft at school reported to teacher
Fear of reprisals	Physical attack

The 1996 British Crime Survey turned the question around and asked victims why they did report the crime to the police. The reasons given include: obligation to report (duty to report), it was a serious crime, stops repeat of crime to others, advantages to victim (recovering of property), for insurance claim, needed police assistance, stops re-victimization by same criminal, retributive motive (catch and punish offender).

Commentary

Leaving aside the actual figures for crime, what victim surveys show is that criminal victimization is 'extremely rare' and crimes of violence 'extremely uncommon' (Sparks, 1981). Statistically, the 'average' person faces the risk of a burglary once every 40 years and being the victim of robbery once every 500 years (Hough and Mayhew, 1983).

Prevalence of victimization

Criminal victimization is not an evenly distributed experience; there are some individuals who suffer much more than others. Thus we can talk about the prevalence of victimization (the crime figures based on those who experience crime), while the incidence of crime is the amount of crime divided by the whole population. So the prevalence of victimization figures show, for example, more burglaries in inner city areas, with young males as the victims of assault (see Table 3.4, below).

Table 3.4: 1998 British Crime Survey

Risk factors in victims of burglary:
- young head of household
- lone adults
- unemployed head of household
- low income household
- living in rented accommodation
- flat or end of terrace house
- home empty for three hours or more during the day
- inner city or council estate residence
- living in north of country
- multi-ethnic area.

Risk factors for repeated victims of burglary:
- single parents
- living in rented accommodation
- living in an inner city area or on a council estate
- living in an area with high physical disorder.

Risk factors in victims of violence:
- single and living alone
- unemployed or low income
- living in rented accommodation
- living in a flat or terraced house
- go out often
- living in London or Northern England.

Risk factors for repeat victims of violence:
- 25–44 year old female
- single parents
- living in rented accommodation or on a council estate.

Source: Mirlees-Black *et al*, 1998.

Some research has tried to establish whether there is a certain type of person who becomes a regular victim. Chambers (1995) suggests the case of individuals from violent homes with low self-esteem, who seem to put themselves in risky situations. For example, such a man may walk through a gang of men standing on a street corner rather than cross the road. Such an action is taken as provocative, and the man is beaten up.

For some women in domestic violence cases, they are attracted to power and so end up in abusive relationships. These women often have low self-esteem and believe the abuse is a sign of love. However, this is a controversial idea and certainly does not explain all domestic violence and abuse.

Based on the data from the British Crime Surveys, Dowd (quoted in Hollin, 1992) has analysed the experience of violent criminal victimization for men and women. Women experience six main types of violence (in order of importance).

- Domestic violence – assaulted at home by a partner or ex-partner.
- Leisure-related – occurs where the victim spends their leisure time (for example, pub).
- Occupational hazard – as part of work (for example, nurses assaulted by patients).
- Friend/neighbour disputes
- Provocation – the victim is responsible for the violence herself (for example, attacks someone who fights back).
- Defended/chased – defence against attack.

Dowd also noted the six types of male violent victimization (in order of importance).

- Pub fights.
- Fights between friends.
- Occupational hazard.
- Minor fracas.
- Serious unprovoked wounding.
- Domestic violence.

Fear of crime

The Figgie Report (1980) in the USA distinguishes between two types of fear: concrete fear (fear of being a victim of a specific crime), and formless fear (a general feeling of being unsafe). Some 46% of women had high levels of concrete fear and 48% had formless fear. For men, it was 34% and 26% respectively.

However, the perceptions of crime and the fear of it generally would give the impression that the risks are greater for the 'average' person. Hough and Mayhew (1985) found in the 1984 British Crime Survey that 23% of the respondents were 'very worried' about burglary and 20% about muggings. By the 1996 British Crime Survey (Mirlees-Black *et al*, 1996) those 'very worried' about burglary accounted for 22% and for muggings, 19%. Further

analysis of the results showed that women are more fearful than men (see Table 3.5, below): 16–30 year olds are the most fearful age group and those living in inner cities are most worried about muggings.

Commentary

The group traditionally with the most fear of muggings is elderly women, who are the least attacked. Meanwhile, young males are the least afraid, but the most attacked.

Table 3.5: Fear of violence

	Men	Women
Afraid to go out alone at night	11%	57%
Afraid of being mugged	39%	56%
Afraid of being attacked in their own homes	27%	55%
Afraid of using public transport at night	11%	35%
Afraid of some other form of attack	21%	27%

Source: 'Battered Britain', 1995.

Looking at how people view crime, there is evidence of contradictory beliefs. Many people see the crime rates as rising generally and overstate the risks, but when asked about crime in their area, they understate the problem even in areas of high crime rates. Bottoms *et al* (1981) focused on the so-called 'red light area' of Sheffield, which has a very high crime rate for the city. Some 54% of the residents of this area who were interviewed felt that the crime rate was the same as the average for the city.

Similarly there are contradictions in what people worry about. British Crime Surveys show that respondents are more worried about assaults than road accidents. Yet there are over 50 times more deaths and serious injuries from road accidents than from assaults (see Table 3.6, below).

Table 3.6: Crime still heads list of people's anxieties

Comparing the results of the 1994 British Crime Survey with earlier surveys shows that people are still 'very worried' about becoming a victim. In fact, this is a greater worry than losing their jobs, illness in the family or being injured in a road accident.

But the fear of crime is not necessarily linked to actual crime. The fear of being a burglary victim has not changed, though the burglary rate has doubled since 1984.

Less than 2% of the 16,500 people interviewed say they never go out after dark because of the fear of crime, but more people do change their lives to avoid certain places.

Percent of who replied 'very worried'

Home accident	11
Bombs/terrorist attacks	12
Debt	12
Illness	14
Mugging	21
Job loss	21
Road accident	22
Burglary	26

Source: adapted from the *Guardian*, 1996.

Research has also shown that the fear of crime can be influenced by the amount of television watched. Gerbner and Gross (1976) found that heavy television viewers were more likely to overestimate the chances of encountering violence, and were less trusting of people generally. The stereotypical image of criminals emphasized by television is the 'evil stranger', but many women will suffer victimization at the hands of someone they know (Madriz, 1997).

McCabe and Raine (1997) found that fear of crime produced the same psychological effects as being a victim, though to a lower degree. Those fearful of crime report stress, depression and sleeping difficulties.

Effects of victimization

With most minor crimes the main effect is a financial loss and the consequent anger at the inconvenience of the loss. Usually, preventative measures are then taken.

Criminal victimization can have effects on physical health. For example, there is a lot of work in the USA on the permanent disabilities from gunshot wounds among the young. Meanwhile, in the UK many 'joy riders' end up in hospital.

KEY STUDY 6

Researcher: Riordan (1999)

Aim: To understand how female victims experience indecent exposure, and the impact on general fears of sexual crime.

Method: 72 questionnaires distributed to postgraduate students, university administration staff, city council employees, and women living on a particular estate, all in the East Midlands.

Results: 35 respondents had been victims of indecent exposure once; seven had experienced more than once; one victim five times. Initial reactions: shock (48.6%), amusement (34.3%), fear (25.7%), disgust (5.7%) and annoyance (2.9%). Perception of danger: 23 victims and 26 non-victims considered exposers dangerous; 80% of the victims were concerned about what would follow the exposure. Attitudes to sexual crime: ten victims had increased fear since the exposure; ten victims had changed their behaviours in some way because of the exposure.

Conclusions: ' ...the experience of indecent exposure is likely to reinforce those fears (of sexual crime) rather than to exacerbate them. It is not in any sense a trivial offence' (p. 315).

It is important to note that even apparently trivial crimes can have some long-term effects on the victim (see Key Study 6). But serious crimes have the greatest psychological effect on the victim. For example, Resnick and Markaway (1991) summarize the effects of sexual attacks on women to show a pattern of responses.

- Immediately after attack – feelings of confusion, fear and worry with physical reactions like shaking.
- First few hours – feelings of depression, exhaustion and restlessness.
- First week after attack – distress still high.
- Two to three weeks after attack – distress declines in second week, but then peaks in third week.
- Two to three months after attack – positive readjustment usually, but fear, anxiety and personal difficulties (for example, with relationships) still there.
- Long-term effects – decline in social activities; in some cases severe problems like post-traumatic stress disorder, even leading to suicide.

Real Life Application 12:

Victims of violence

Everybody thinks they are safe. But tomorrow anyone could be a victim. The greatest effect is psychological, not the financial loss.

The recovery of the crime victim is often compared with the stages of bereavement. The first phase is immediate feelings of shock, numbness and disorientation. There is a feeling of disbelief and of being vulnerable. It is important for the victim to have support at this stage.

Then in the second stage, the victim attempts to pick up the pieces (literally and metaphorically). They may experience sadness, anger, fear, guilt and self-pity.

The final stage is when the experience is assimilated into the victim's life and they can return to their 'normal' lives (if that is ever now possible). The length of these stages varies from individual to individual.

Source: *Woman's Journal*, 1988.

Summary

- The effect of victimization has a series of stages, and could be likened to bereavement.

Questions

1 What are some of the key factors that influence the seriousness of the effect of victimization?
2 Is the experience of victimization different for men and women?
3 What psychological factors help victims to recover more quickly from their experience of victimization?

Post-traumatic stress disorder

In some cases, especially involving violence, the victim may develop post-traumatic stress disorder. This was first diagnosed in American soldiers returning from the war in Vietnam and is now recognized in the classification systems of mental illness. Originally, the diagnosis was used only for post-combat soldiers, but now it is widely acknowledged to occur in other situations, including violent criminal victimization. For example, Kilpatrick *et al* (1987) investigated around 300 female crime victims (of whom half had been sexually assaulted) and found that a quarter had, or were experiencing, post-traumatic stress disorder (as defined by DSM III in the USA). This is now specifically called 'Rape Trauma Syndrome' (see Figure 3.1, below).

Figure 3.1: Rape trauma syndrome

Physical	Psychological	Behavioural
Insomnia/ nightmares	Depression/ tearfulness	Inability to go out
Poor appetite/ weight loss/ swallowing and eating problems	Anxiety, flashbacks, guilt and self-blame	Avoidance of rape-related stimuli; social withdrawal
Menstrual irregularities	Decline in sexual enjoyment	Increasing dependence on others
Difficulty in micturation (urinating)	Poor concentration	Alcohol/drug abuse
General non-specific complaints: weakness/ dizziness/ general malaise/ faintness/nausea/ increased muscle tension	Irritability and apathy, phobias	Moving house/cutting off phone NB: Pregnancy/sexually transmitted disease/AIDS risks

Source: Mezey, 1988.

Specific symptoms must be present for the diagnosis of post-traumatic stress disorder. These include the following.

- Intrusive thoughts – re-experiencing flashbacks, nightmares, generally unable to stop thinking about the event.
- Avoidant behaviour – avoiding situations that may trigger memories of the event, loss of interest in any pleasurable activities, feelings of numbness in response to everything.
- Feelings – pointlessness, increased anxiety, fear of the event happening again, shame, guilt and bitterness.
- Behaviour – inability to make decisions, irritability, lack of concentration, anger and sometimes violent outbursts.
- Physical effects – physical illness, depression, hyperactivity and high stress reactions, increased smoking, drinking or drug use.

Certain features of the violence have been found to increase the psychological distress: if the assault is sexual, if there is stalking involved, if the victim is homeless or a drug abuser, if the victim was already anxious or depressed (Robinson *et al*, 1998).

Weaver and Clum (1995) found that self-blame

by the victim and the perception of a threat to life were more important in the development of psychological distress than actual physical injury.

MacLeod and Paton (1999) see the post-event cognitions of the victim as key to the recovery. These include the following.

- Blame attribution – self-blame actually encourages the victim to feel that they must avoid similar incidents in the future.
- Perceived control – feeling that they have control of future situations is important. But self-blame with low feelings of control leads to a fall in self-esteem, and problems with recovery.
- Counterfactual thinking – the process of mentally undoing the event to produce a better outcome (counterfactual thinking) is only helpful if the victim has perceived control over future such events.

But there are many victims of violence who do not develop post-traumatic stress disorder.

Commentary

In a different vein, Pollock (1999) found that 52% of murderers assessed in a special hospital could be classed as suffering from post-traumatic stress disorder.

Victims of abuse

There is plenty of evidence that victims of abuse as children have more psychiatric problems as adults as well as greater drug and alcohol misuse. For example, Schultz (1986, quoted in Zimbardo *et al*, 1995) found that 98% of adults with multiple personality disorder and 54% of those with major depression had experienced childhood abuse.

Another area often overlooked is the victims of business crime like fraud. In many cases, the victims are not aware of being victimized.

Criminal negligence leading to workplace injuries and deaths leaves its victims, too (Zedner, 1994).

An entirely different effect of victimization is the financial costs. Some attempts at estimates have been made. For example, Robinson *et al* (1998) quote an estimate of £189 million to the health service for treating the physical injuries of domestic violence victims in Greater London in 1996.

Commentary

The 1996 British Crime Survey estimates the average cost of burglary as £370. This varies between £100 for an attempted burglary (that is, repairing windows and so on) to £620 when something is stolen. Theft from a car costs the victim an average of £290.

Secondary victimization

There is a wider impact of victimization. This is known as secondary or indirect victimization (for example, families of murder victims). Though the family members were not attacked, they suffer the consequences of the sudden bereavement.

Based on interviews with 80 families, Brown *et al* (1990) outline the problems faced by the families of the murder victim.

- Sudden arrival of the police with the news.
- In certain cases, hearing the news through the media.
- Practical problems if the home is sealed as a crime scene.
- Emotional problems following the re-opening of the home.
- Formal identification of the body.
- Inquests and court proceedings including hearing intimate details of the murder.

Even witnesses or bystanders of serious crimes can be classed as secondary victims.

Morgan and Zedner (1992) also emphasise that children suffer, and are mostly overlooked as victims (for example, a third of burglaries are in houses where children live).

Victim–offender interaction

One way of looking at victimization is to see it as an interaction. Thus the victim influences the offender and vice versa. Using this idea, Luckenbill (1977) has focused on violent acts that end in murder. The interaction can be classed as a series of 'transactions'.

- The interaction begins with the victim making a comment, refusing to comply with a request, or flirting with another person. This can be a direct provocation or interpreted as so by the offender.
- The offender checks the perception of the provocation. For example, if it is a verbal comment, the offender may ask, 'What did you say?'
- The offender decides not to retreat by challenging the victim with verbal comments or threats.
- The victim then counter-attacks verbally or physically. Luckenbill argues that this behaviour confirms to the offender that violence is an appropriate behaviour here.
- The offender attacks and the murder is committed.

This analysis does suggest that the murder is 'victim-precipitated'. There are many cases of murder which are not so.

Commentary

Whether the victim of any crime knows the offender or not can be important. Using data from the British Crime Survey, Mawby and Gill (1987) asked victims if they were affected by the crime. Some 29% replied 'very much' or 'quite a lot' if the offender had been a stranger, but this increased to 40% for a casual acquaintance, and 53% if the offender was well known to them (like a spouse).

Helping the victim

The victim's needs for help will vary with social support, personality differences and the ability to communicate his or her needs. For example, educated individuals usually seek out practical help. Thus there are groups of victims whose needs are not being met because they do not express them or do not seek help.

Victims often need practical help in the short term, like mending of broken windows after a burglary. But research has also found that many victims like to be kept informed about the progress of their case. In the UK, The Victim's Charter attempts to encourage the police to do this. On a more organized front, 'victim movements' have developed in many countries.

These groups try to provide help for victims in an organized fashion, as well as work as a pressure group for 'victim's rights'. The assumption behind this type of help is that victims are likely to be traumatized and need such help from those who can understand (that is, fellow sufferers). This is sometimes called 'crisis intervention'. The victim support group may, in fact, make the first move. Maguire and Corbett (1987) found that 90% of victims who received an unsolicited visit were happy to talk compared to only 7% for an unsolicited letter.

Two areas of crime that have good histories of victim support are domestic violence, and 'rape crisis centres'. Initially the support has come from the 'women's movement'. In 1972, Erin Pizzey set up the first women's refuge for battered women in Chiswick, London. It was actually a place where the women could escape to, and live for a while. There are over 100 refuges in Britain today.

The first 'rape crisis centres' were opened in London in 1976, and in Birmingham in 1979. There are around 50 such centres today in Britain. They are reliant, in the main, on volunteers providing a 24-hour telephone helpline, and face-to-face counselling. Many also try to educate, and prefer to talk of 'survivors' rather than victims.

Corbett and Hobdell (1988) believe that 'rape crisis centres' have five aims:

- To help victims regain control over their lives through expression of the experience.
- To reassure the victim that her response is not abnormal.
- To recognize that rape also affects those close to the woman (such as family and friends).
- Giving practical assistance – for example, accompanying the victim to visit special clinics.
- Assisting women who must give evidence in court.

The above are all undertaken by voluntary help. The State provides a means of financial compensation through the Criminal Injuries Board and compensation orders by the courts.

Essay Questions

1 'Eye-witness memory is not accurate.' Discuss.
2 Discuss the methods used by the police to help the eye-witness recall the event. Which methods are most effective?
3 What is the British Crime Survey? Discuss what can be learnt about the experience of criminal victimization from this survey.

4 The legal system

This chapter concentrates on the psychological aspects of the legal system and tackles three main themes: the trial itself, child witnesses, and offender punishment and rehabilitiation. Real Life Applications that are considered are:

- RLA 13: Jurors' right to know
- RLA 14: Banged up

In the section that follows we will focus on the psychology of the trial process, the perception of witnesses, the influence of laywers and the jury decision-making process.

The trial

The whole of the trial is a social situation with formal and informal interactions involved (see Table 4.1, below). This means that there are many psychological processes at work at each stage, other than the legal aspects of the trial.

Table 4.1: Stages in the trial process

Indictment
Defendant's plea
Prosecution opening statement
Defence opening statement
Witnesses
Defence closing arguments
Prosecution closing arguments
Judge's instructions on procedures
Jury decision
Judge sentencing (if accused found guilty)

The jury decision can be influenced by three main aspects of the trial: pre-trial and trial influences and procedures, perception of the evidence and witnesses, and the work of the prosecution and defence lawyers.

Pre-trial influences

The most important extra-evidential influence is pre-trial publicity (PTP). This can be divided into two types: *factual* (including details of past criminal record of the defendant), and *emotive* (assuming guilt before the trial). Both types affect the juror's view of the evidence. In fact, Timothy McVeigh

(known as the Oklahoma Bomber) appealed in 1997 against his death sentence on the grounds of 'emotive' PTP.

In high-profile cases, it is almost impossible for the jurors to have not seen the PTP. Using newspaper cuttings with a mock jury, Linz and Penrod (1992) found that PTP, including prior convictions and 'sensational' reporting, impacted on the jury decision. There is a legal question of whether jurors should know about the prior convictions of the defendant (see RLA 13, below).

Padawer-Singer and Barton (1974) found 50% more 'guilty' decisions by jurors aware of a past criminal record and a retracted confession of the defendant, compared to not knowing this information. The judge's instructions to ignore this has little effect.

Commentary

Fein *et al* (1997) set up mock juries using the PTP from the OJ Simpson case. It was biased against the defendant and in some cases mentioned his African-American race. On the whole, the jurors tended to vote 'guilty' (around 80%), unless they knew the race of the defendant, and then they discounted the PTP as racist, (only 45% of the jurors voted 'guilty' in this case).

Real Life Application 13: Jurors' right to know

Simon Berkowitz was cleared of burglary at Paddy Ashdown's solicitors' office without the jury knowing that Berkowitz had 230 previous convictions for burglary. The judge had refused the use of previous convictions as evidence because it would be prejudicial. But why does the English legal system not allow the inclusion of previous convictions?

The evidence supports such a move. Statistics show that offenders tend to re-offend, particularly for certain crimes like sexual crimes. Some cases are presented in a misleading way if previous convictions are hidden. For example, Colin James Evans set up a childminding business and was accused of abusing the children. He was acquitted because the impression given at the trial was of a man trying to help, but hindered by false accusations. However, Evans was a convicted child molester. If the jury had known this fact, they would have convicted him.

Source: JR Spencer; adapted from *The Times*, 1992.

Summary

• The author is arguing that many suspects in court are re-offenders, and for the jury not to know that the suspects have a past criminal record distorts the impression of the suspect.

Questions

1 What type of pre-trial publicity is a suspect's past criminal record?
2 If the newspapers report that a suspect has a past criminal record, the judge can ask the jury to ignore such facts. How much influence will such a request by the judge have on the juries decision?
3 What other pre-trial publicity can be prejudicial to the case?

Trial influences on decisions

Within the trial itself, there are a number of influences on jury decisions. One is the inclusion of non-evidence. This is evidence that the judge decides is legally inadmissible. In other words, it is presented to the jury, then the decision is made that it cannot be included. Wolf and Montgomery (1977) found that this type of evidence, which should be ignored, is noticed most by the jury.

A key influence is the judge's instructions during the case. Generally research has shown that many juries are confused by the legal technicalities. Elwork *et al* (1981) showed mock jurors a video-taped trial including the judge's instructions. Over

one-third of the jurors made the incorrect legal verdict. When the judge's instructions were clarified, the incorrect verdicts dropped to around 10%.

Instructions given before the case began had a better effect on the juries' ability to integrate facts and the law. Overall, however, written instructions are better than verbal ones.

Commentary

Research has found that the charges themselves can influence the jury's decision. Individuals were more likely to be found guilty of specific charges if considered with other charges than alone (Tanford and Penrod, 1982).

Perception of the witness

The most important part of the trial is the evidence provided by witnesses. The accuracy of the evidence provided by witnesses is discussed elsewhere (see page 43–51), but what is the impact on the jury of the witnesses' evidence? In one of her experiments with mock juries, Loftus (1974) showed that witness evidence is very powerful in the mind of the jury, and is only slightly diminished by discrediting the witness (see Key Study 7, below). This is also evidence of the perseverance effect – the tendency to believe the first thing people are told, even if it is later contradicted.

KEY STUDY 7	
Researcher:	Loftus (1974)
Aim:	To show the importance of eye-witness testimony in the mind of jurors.
Method:	Some 150 mock jurors heard about a robbery and murder at a local store. There were three conditions, each varying the presence of a witness: (1) a witness who saw a man leaving the store; (2) no witness; (3) a witness who was later shown to have poor eyesight.
Results:	In condition (1) 72% of the mock jurors found the defendant guilty compared to 18% in condition (2). But in condition (3), 68% still believed the defendant guilty.
Conclusions:	Jurors place too much emphasis on witnesses whether they are accurate or not.

As well as the faith placed in witnesses by juries, there are also the general principles of impression formation of witnesses. For example, when witnesses are perceived as likeable, they are seen as more credible, whether working for the defence or the prosecution. Garcia and Griffit (1978) varied the likeability of the witnesses in a mock crime about a car accident (see Table 4.2, below).

Table 4.2: Summary of results from Garcia and Griffit (1978)

Likeability of Prosecution	Defence	Mean rating of guilt
Positive	Positive	3.25
Positive	Negative	4.10
Negative	Positive	2.50
Negative	Negative	3.45

Another factor in the impression of witnesses is the language they use. Lakoff (1975) has highlighted what could be called 'powerless language'. This would include a high frequency of 'hedges' (for example, 'I think' and 'perhaps'), and answering direct questions in an unsure way (for example, with rising intonation at the end of the sentence). Witnesses of either gender using this type of language were perceived as less intelligent, less competent, less likeable and less believable (O'Barr and Conley, 1976). However, witnesses are perceived as more competent if their accent is standard English.

Commentary

The nature of the witness's evidence is important. Positive identification has a greater impact than negative testimony and identification.

Witness confidence

Juries are also influenced by the confidence of the witness, though research has shown that the level of confidence of accuracy of recall is not related to actual accuracy of recall.

The coherence of the testimony is also important. In other words, if witnesses are clear and organized in their testimony it is perceived as true – including the speed of answer and specific details given. However, neither factor is linked to accuracy of recall in reality.

Commentary

Juries are influenced by the following characteristics of the witness: likeability, language used, accent, positive or negative testimony, confidence and coherence of evidence.

Perception of the evidence

The evidence presented in court can be complex, and often the trial lasts a long time. How do the jurors make sense of the trial and perceive the evidence presented? Pennington and Hastie (1990) have proposed the 'story model' (see Figure 4.1, below).

This suggests that jurors attempt to make sense of the entirety of the evidence by imposing a summary structure ('story'). Then they seek the best fit between the verdict and their 'story'. So, in practice, the 'story' mediates between the evidence and the final decision. The juror is not just hearing the evidence, but is trying to make sense of everything within a conceptual framework.

The juror is actively constructing a version of what happened. This is no different to how we actively construct memories and events in our and others' everyday lives.

Figure 4.1: 'Story model' for jury decision-making (Pennington and Hastie, 1990)

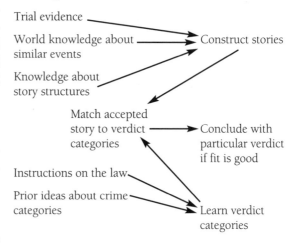

However, what makes the situation different to everyday life is that there are competing stories. The prosecution and the defence are each trying to create their own versions of what happened. Often, though, the failure to comprehend and recall relevant facts can lead to deviant verdicts. Using mock juries with a murder trial on video, Hastie *et al* (1983) offered five possible verdicts. In reality, only one verdict was possible from the evidence. The researchers then analysed the jurors who chose the other verdicts and found errors in comprehension (of, for example, the legal technicalities) and recall (of the witnesses' testimonies).

The role of attribution

In the same way that individuals make attributions about the cause of behaviour in everyday life, so jurors will follow the same cognitive processes in attributing the cause of the crimes. For example, Walster (1966) found that individuals vary their attribution of blame for an accident depending on the amount of damage or injury involved. If there is a large amount of damage or injury, then it is more likely that a dispositional attribution will be made. This is the belief that the individual is directly to blame for the accident, whereas a situational attribution tends to blame the situation as the cause of the event.

The hindsight effect

Another attribution process is known as the hindsight effect. This is the tendency to blame the victim for what happened after the event. In an experiment, Janoff-Bulman et al (quoted in Sabini, 1995) gave students a story about dating which ended either with or without a rape. In the case of the rape ending, the participants tended to believe that the rape could have been predicted and placed greater blame on the victim (for example, in the way in which the woman dressed or her behaviour).

Commentary

Peacock et al (1997) set up mock juries with American students during the OJ Simpson trial. They noticed that the decision about guilt was based on the cognitive balance theory (Heider, 1958). This involves the belief of guilt, then the interpretation of evidence to balance with the guilt or not – for example, the belief in the legal system as biased against Simpson or not. Also the role of direct experience of battered women influenced the decision.

Expert witness

Many trials employ expert witnesses to help clarify complex issues. Experts warning the jury about the reliability of certain witness evidence does reduce the trust in such evidence, but does not necessarily improve the ability to discriminate between 'good' and 'bad' evidence (Hollin, 1989). Psychologists are often used as expert witnesses, particularly in the USA. Their role can be divided into four parts (Haward, 1981)

- Experimental – the job of the psychologist here is to inform the court of relevant psychological research to the case, like the accuracy of the eye-witness testimony.
- Clinical – this involves a psychological assessment of the defendant. Is the defendant psychologically fit to stand trial or should there be a plea of 'not guilty by reason of insanity'?
- Actuarial – this is similar to the first role, but is more of an estimate of the likelihood of certain behaviours. It is usually based on statistics.
- Advisor – in this case the psychologist is involved with the legal team and advises them. This is quite rare in the UK.

In a survey of around 200 psychologists, the most important type of psychological evidence used in courts in the UK was behaviour assessments or interviews with the defendant, followed by standardized cognitive tests (Gudjonsson, 1985).

Commentary

The text below outlines the 'fors' and 'againsts' of the use of psychologists as expert witnesses.

For

Psychologists have skills beyond the 'ordinary person', including the understanding of the working of memory, or the knowledge of psychometric testing. Common sense views of human behaviour are often wrong, and psychologists can correct these misconceptions. It is a risk to not give testimony (Wells, 1986).

Against

Most psychological research is lab-based experiments, and these conclusions may not generalize to 'real life'. Much research is able to explain behaviour in the past, but not predict future behaviour. In the study of eye-witness testimony, there is often too much focus on the few mistaken identities rather than the many correct identifications (Konecni and Ebbesen, 1986).

Complex expert evidence

Harrower (1998) highlights the problem for jurors of complex expert evidence, with the example of the Louise Woodward case. (Woodward, who is British, was accused of murdering the baby son of the family for whom she was working as an au pair in the USA.) Both defence and prosecution used expert medical opinion about the death of the baby Woodward was caring for. The jury made a surprising 'guilty' verdict, which the judge later overturned. The jury was accused of being influenced by other factors because they could not understand the expert evidence.

Jurors are also aware of what they believe to be right and wrong. For example, after the miner's strike in 1985 in the north of England, juries convicted few miners accused of rioting. Here the jury 'can be seen as reflecting social opinions about the nature of right and wrong, rather than upholding a purely legal perspective' (McClintock, 1997, p. 123).

Commentary

The perception of evidence by the jury is influenced by: its complexity, the testimony of expert witnesses, attributions of the cause of the crime made by jurors, and the 'story' they impose on the trial as it unfolds.

Prosecution versus defence

The task of the opposing counsels is to persuade the jury that their version of the events is true. There are a number of factors involved in the process of persuasion. The general model of persuasion takes into account three factors: who is doing the persuading (the source), what they are saying (the message), and who is being persuaded (the recipient). For each factor, there will be a number of influences.

The source

Important factors here include: the use of an expert, the attractiveness of the source, and his/her trustworthiness. This last factor is most influential if the source appears to be arguing against his/her own self-interests. Judges arguing for lenient penalties for juvenile delinquents have a more persuasive effect than drug-dealers arguing the same way (Kelman and Hovland, 1953). Similarly a habitual criminal arguing for stricter sentences is more persuasive than a lawyer (Walster *et al*, 1966).

The message

The content of the message can include both sides or only one side of the argument. The most important factor here is the order of presentation of arguments and evidence. Pennington (1982) set up mock rape trials and varied the order of presentation of the arguments. In one condition, the defence case came first, followed immediately by the prosecution. In this situation, the defence case tended to win more often. This is known as the primacy effect – the importance of the first piece of information. But if there was a large interval between the two arguments (like an overnight recess), then the prosecution won more times. This is known as the recency effect – where the last piece of information is more influential (see Table 4.3, next column).

Table 4.3: The primacy and recency effects

First speech	Interval	Second speech	Verdict
Prosecution	No	Defence	Guilty (primary effect)
Defence	No	Prosecution	Not guilty (primary effect)
Defence	Large	Prosecution	Guilty (recency effect)
Prosecution	Large	Defence	Not guilty (recency effect)

What about the quality of the arguments used by the lawyers? This is only applicable when the individuals are highly involved (that is, they feel that it is relevant to them). Axsom *et al* (1987) played tapes of discussions about prisoners and probation. The researchers varied the level of involvement of the participants and the quality of the arguments, (with the audience cheering or booing on the tapes). Those participants with low involvement were more influenced by the audience than the quality of the arguments.

The recipient

The key variable in persuasion here is the latitude of rejection or acceptance. In other words, how large an attitude change is the recipient being asked to make? The smaller the change, the more likely it is that persuasion will be effective. So where the guilt appears obvious to the jury, it is very difficult for the defence to persuade them because 'not guilty' is outside their latitude of acceptance.

Jury decision-making

Jury decisions are influenced by three groups of factors: jury composition, the decision-making process, and the characteristics of the defendant (see Table 4.4, page 63).

Jury selection and composition

In the UK, juries are made up of twelve people for criminal cases. These people are chosen randomly from the electorate. Thus, no qualifications are required. The decision-making process is undertaken in secret and there is no evaluation of the verdict given. However, legally a decision must be made.

Commentary

The selection of the twelve jurors is not, in fact, completely random because the opposing legal counsels can object to individual jurors based on their personalities,

Table 4.4: The jury

Jury composition	Decision-making process
Size of jury	Majority influence/conformity
Characteristics/attitudes that influence verdict	Group polarization
Influence within jury	'Groupthink'
	Emergence of leader
	Social 'loafing'

Characteristics of defendant

Stereotyping process

Physical attractiveness

Race

Accent

attitudes or beliefs. This is known as peremptory challenges in Britain, and 'voir dire' in the USA. How the lawyers decide on who to oppose is based on the principles of impression formation. In other words, they form an initial impression of what the person is like in the same way that anyone does at a first meeting. Lawyers tend to have their 'pet ideas' on who to choose.

Individual differences within juries

But specific research into juror variables (like gender, age, race, occupation or personality) found that they are not related to juror decisions. In other words, the verdict cannot be predicted from the make-up of the jury. Research into juries in Birmingham by Baldwin and McConville (1979) believed that 'no single social factor', including social class, led to significant effects on the verdicts returned.

However, one personality type that does seem to influence jury decisions is the 'authoritarian personality' type. This is a personality type who is very narrow-minded, against change and holds strict conservative views. It is usually measured using a questionnaire called the 'California F Scale'.

Using the OJ Simpson trial, Chapdelaine and Griffin (1997) found a correlation between the 'California F Scale' and the belief in Simpson's guilt, the perception of the fairness of the trial and the severity of the recommended sentence. Thus, the 'authoritarian personality' type were more likely to see Simpson as guilty, believe the trial was fair and recommend longer sentences. However, overall, the decisions were based on an appropriate sentence for Simpson rather than the general belief of guilt.

Other research has found that in the USA the juror's attitude towards the death penalty is a key variable in jury decision-making. It is probable that

an 'authoritarian personality' type would favour the death penalty.

In a mock murder trial experiment, Ellsworth (1993) used jury-eligible California residents and showed them part of a video of a police officer's and the defendant's testimony in an assault trial. Ellsworth found that supporters of the death penalty were more likely to vote guilty immediately before jury deliberations had taken place. Ellsworth argues that attitudes come in a 'bundle'. Death penalty supporters tended to show more trust in police practices and to be more sceptical of the defendant's case, compared to those opposed to the death penalty (see Table 4.5, below).

Table 4.5: Summary of the results from Ellsworth (1993)
Mean evaluation of evidence by supporters and non-supporters of the death penalty

	Supporters	Non-supporters
Officer's truthfulness	4.55	3.44*
Defendant's truthfulness	3.69	3.05
Accuracy of witnesses	4.35	3.25**

Scale ranged from 1 to 6; higher number indicates more favourable to evaluation

* = significant difference at p0.05; ** = p0.01

Other research has found that there is a positive correlation between the trial experience of the juror and the severity of the sentence, irrelevant of the type of prior experience. There is a limited amount of research suggesting that men are less likely to convict a rapist.

Among the jury members, those of higher occupational status were more involved and more influential. Hastie *et al* (1983) set up 69 mock juries and found that the most talkative were dominant in the group – and these were more often male. The 34–56 age group was also seen as more influential.

Commentary

Where the background of jurors may influence their views is in their reaction to the evidence. For example, jurors from certain areas (like inner cities) may not be surprised or see it as unusual that the defendant was carrying a weapon.

Decision-making process

The difficulty with research in this area is that it is illegal to study the jury at work or question jurors afterwards. This means that any research must be with mock juries. It is generally assumed that the jury decision-making process is similar to that of any small group making decisions.

The decision-making process of any group passes through three stages which can be applied to juries (Hastie *et al*, 1983).

- 'Orientation process' – an agenda is set and the evidence is explored.
- 'Open conflict' – where differences of opinion become obvious and there is a focus on disputed evidence. This tends to be a move from facts to emotions.
- 'Reconciliation' – either the conflict is resolved and a verdict is given or the majority attempt to persuade the others. The main point is that attempts are made to reduce any previous conflicts.

In the main, the majority opinion tends to predominate. For example, Kalven and Zeisel (1966) found that of 215 juries with a majority view at the beginning of the deliberations, only six changed to the minority decision by the end of the discussions. But there is evidence of a 'leniency bias' to favour the defendant, the longer are the deliberations. So if there is disagreement, it is easier to persuade jurors of a not-guilty than a guilty verdict during the deliberations.

Currently, juries are required to reach unanimous decisions (that is, they all agree on the verdict). This could take longer than a majority verdict (for example, 10:2), and so increase the possibility of 'leniency bias'.

Hastie *et al* (1983) set up mock juries of a murder trial, but divided them into three conditions. They had to make a 12:0, a 10:2 or an 8:4 decision. All the proceedings were videotaped. It was found that for the two conditions with a majority-only verdict, discussions were shorter and the majority jurors were more bullying in their persuasive style. Thus, unanimous verdicts may have benefits for justice.

Commentary

There seems to be no difference in the size of the jury as to whether it is more effective in the decisions made. Work with mock juries finds that six- and twelve-person juries come to the same verdicts.

Jurors and conformity

Experiments with mock juries find that if two-thirds of the group agree, then that decision will eventually win. Any less, and the group becomes deadlocked. Generally in psychology it has been of interest how the majority win through. The research on conformity pressures show that the minority will change for a number of reasons.

Conformity is when an individual gives up his or her personal views under group pressure. Within a jury situation, two types of conformity may occur: normative and informational. In the latter case, the individual conforms to the group norms because he/she does not know what to do and looks to the group for guidance. It may be that the individual does not understand the legal technicalities of the case. With normative conformity, the individual outwardly conforms to avoid rejection by the group or to gain rewards from them, but inwardly disagrees. This is a more superficial form of conformity.

The classic study of normative conformity was undertaken by Solomon Asch in the 1950s. He asked individuals to say in front of a group of people which two out of four drawn lines were the same length. The answer was obvious. But a number of the group members deliberately gave the wrong answer. Would the 'real participants' (the others in the group were working for the experimenter) follow their own judgements and give the obvious correct answer or conform to the group with the wrong answer? The participants conformed in about one-third of the trials.

Asch (1951) developed this experiment to pin down the factors involved in conformity. He found the best group size to gain conformity was 7:1. Also, greater conformity was produced by the more difficult the task, or the higher the status of group members.

This idea of conformity to the majority was dominant until Moscovici (1976) showed that the minority could influence the whole group. In a series of artificial experiments, Moscovici found that a minority of two (in a group of six) could change the whole group if they were consistent in their arguments (and did not waver). Further research has shown that the minority influence applies if the individuals appear to be making a sacrifice, are acting to principles not ulterior motives, and combine both flexibility and consistency in their views (Hogg and Vaughan, 1995).

In an experiment with mock juries, Nemeth (1977) compared whether the majority or minority wins if they are advocating 'guilty' or 'not guilty' verdicts. When the majority was advocating 'not guilty', this view won on sixteen out of eighteen occasions. But if the majority view was 'guilty', this view won on seven occasions out of nineteen, with the jury being undecided five times.

Commentary

Whether the minority or majority view wins depends on who is arguing with the general social consensus. For example, when the minority view is the social consensus, then they have a better chance of winning, and the same with the majority.

Group polarization

Another decision-making process observed in groups is known as group polarization. Stoner (1961) was the first to experimentally study group polarization, but it was called 'risky shift' at that time. Participants were given twelve dilemmas to think about by themselves, then asked as a group to discuss the dilemmas. Stoner found that the group decisions were riskier than the individual decisions. Later research noted that the group decision would sometimes be more cautious.

Moscovici and Zavalloni (1969) coined the phrase 'group polarization' to show that group decisions would always be more extreme (either riskier or more cautious) than the individual decisions (see Figure 4.2, below).

Figure 4.2: Examples of dilemma to test group polarization

You are a member of a jury and there is ambiguity in the evidence to convict a particular defendant. You are tending to feel that the defendant is 'not guilty'. At what level of risk would you decide to convict? Try the dilemma by yourself first, then discuss it in a small group.

There is a chance that the defendant will commit the same crime again if found 'not guilty'. There is:

1 – a 10% chance they will commit the same crime again

2 – a 30% chance

3 – a 50% chance

4 – a 70% chance

5 – a 90% chance.

Does the decision change if it is a rapist, or a burglar or a child murderer?

Commentary

Group polarization can also be noted with federal judges either sitting as a 'three' or 'one' during a trial. The three judges gave 65% of their judgements as 'libertarian' (less harsh) compared to 30% by the individual judges.

Where group polarization doesn't apply

Generally group polarization does not apply in situations where individuals are arguing for something they believe in. However, the effect is also influenced by identification with the defendant, the victim or the authorities. This process is through the social identity theory, where individuals 'self-stereotype' themselves based on the groups they feel they belong to (Wetherell, 1987). For example, a former police officer on the jury may identify with the police officers giving evidence, and be influenced in his or her verdict that way.

Groupthink

The decision-making process of a group can also show evidence of 'groupthink'. Janis (1972) sees 'groupthink' as the pressure to reach a consensus that leads to an extreme or bizarre decision. This situation could particularly happen to the jury in a long, highly publicized case.

There are certain conditions that facilitate 'groupthink': the group is highly cohesive (that is, it has strong group identity), it is insulated from outside information, it is under pressure to make a decision, all the options are not assessed, the group feels the responsibility in making a very important decision, and there may be a dominant, directive leader.

Commentary

Janis has studied 'groupthink' with political decisions, a famous example being President Kennedy's decision in the 1960s with the Bay of Pigs. This was the area suggested for the invasion of Cuba by American troops, but it was the worst place to do such a thing (because it was marshland).

Psychodynamics

A completely different approach to understanding group decisions comes from psychodynamics. These ideas come from the work of Sigmund Freud and place great emphasis on the unconscious processes in the group. The jury has a task to perform, but it is 'as if another group, comprising the same individuals was operating simultaneously, at the unconscious level' (Morgan and Thomas, 1996).

Thus, the jury decision may be more about these processes than the actual evidence. For example, a jury may convict a child murderer out of the unconscious fear for their children rather than on the evidence. However, this view of the group has little empirical support.

Social loafing

Another area of interest is whether all members of the juries contribute equally to the decision. In a group where there is no individual recognition of effort, research has noted a phenomenon called 'social loafing'. Williams *et al* (1981) define this as a 'reduction in individual effort on a collective task (in which one's outputs are pooled with those of other group members) compared to when working either alone or coactively'.

In a classic experiment, Latane *et al* (1979) asked participants in a sound studio to make as much noise as possible, and the level was measured. First, they did this alone. Then the participants were told that they were linked to other studios and the joint noise levels would be measured. In fact, this was not true. But when the participants thought they were part of a group of six, their individual level of noise dropped by around a quarter, compared to when they believed they were alone. In other words, they were putting in less individual effort to the group cause. Applying this research to the jury situation, the larger the jury, the less individual effort each jury member will put in.

Commentary

Because it is impossible to study real juries, it is assumed that all these psychological processes of groups are at work. A limited number of studies have tried to assess the accuracy of the jury decision by comparing it with the judge's view. In one American study of 3,500 cases, there was around 80% agreement between the judge and jury on the verdict (Kalven and Zeisel, 1966).

Leadership of the jury

Within the jury one psychological process concerns leadership of the group. The jury elects a foreperson. Research has found that the person who is elected as foreperson tends to be of a higher social class, or has previous experience of jury work, or sits at the head of the table or speaks first (Strodtbeck and Lipinski, 1985). In practice, this often means a man. In a San Diego study, Kerr *et al* (1982) found that 90% of forepersons were male, though the majority of jurors were female. However, the foreperson may not be the actual leader of the group.

So who emerges as the leader? General research on leaders has tried to establish if there is a certain type of person who always emerges as the leader. This is known as the 'great person' theory (or originally as the 'great man' theory, because all the research was on male leaders). For example, Mann (1959) reviewed hundreds of studies, but no clear patterns emerged.

Leaderless group discussion

The alternative view is to concentrate on the situational approach and see who emerges as the leader in a particular situation. Experimentally this is tested by the Leaderless Group Discussion (LGD) technique, which involves a group of strangers discussing a particular topic. They are observed to see who emerges as the leader, and group members are asked afterwards who they think became the leader. For example, in highly ambiguous situations (where there is no clear-cut answer), the most talkative individuals emerge as leaders. This is called the 'blabbermouth rule' in some books. However, other research suggests that it is often chance who becomes the leader.

In a LGD experiment, the researchers led some participants to believe that they were making important comments, and these participants emerged as the leaders (whether they were most talkative overall or not).

Characteristics of the defendant

Within law, the characteristics of the defendant (their social identity) are seen as irrelevant to the legal outcome (the sentence given). But psychological research suggests that the social identity of the defendant is very important to the jury.

The jury are often as much influenced by the appearance of the defendant as the evidence. This again follows the pattern of the psychological processes in forming first impressions.

Research on first impressions of individuals has shown that a snap judgement is made, and it is a fairly full impression. In other words, after a brief glimpse of a person, we have decided our whole view of the person, including whether we will like them or not.

Stereotyping

A key part of this process is stereotyping. This involves noticing something about the person and, based on this, attributing them to a particular group of people, then assuming the person has the characteristics of that group. An example might be noticing that the defendant has several tattoos and stereotyping him or her as criminal because it is believed that all criminals have several tattoos.

Lippmann (1922) defines stereotypes as follows: 'For the most part we do not see and then define, we define first and then see. In the great blooming buzzing confusion of the outer world we pick out what our culture has already defined for us and we tend to receive that which we have picked out in the form stereotyped for us by our culture.'

Stereotyping has been shown to influence the recall and interpretation of information. Duncan (1976) showed white American participants a film without sound of two men talking intensely, then one of the men shoved the other. When it was the black man pushing a white man, 75% of the participants perceived the push as violent behaviour, but for the other way around only 17% saw it as violent behaviour.

In another experiment, Snyder and Uranowitz (1978) had participants read the details of the life of 'Betty K', with one of two endings to the story. The story concluded that she was either married or a lesbian. When participants were asked to recall the number of boyfriends she had had at school (a fact not given in the story), the answers were based on the stereotypes. For example, with the lesbian ending, the number of boyfriends recalled was lower. Also participants remembered more of the information consistent with the stereotype.

Commentary

The practical application here is that people may perceive differences and similarities among group members even when they do not exist. It is important to note that these snap judgements and stereotypes are not particularly accurate. However, the juror or lawyer's use of these processes of person perception is the same as impressions made by people everyday.

Key aspects of stereotyping

The text that follows outlines some of the key aspects of stereotyping and snap judgements.

Physical attractiveness
Within society, physical attractiveness is prized highly in both sexes, and such people are treated positively by others. They receive less harsh sentences for the same crime and they do not fit the stereotype of a criminal.

In an experiment, Sigall and Ostrove (1975) asked 120 participants to recommend sentences for burglary or fraud either with or without seeing a photo of the defendant. The photos were either physically attractive or unattractive. The physically attractive photo received shorter sentences (see Table 4.6, next column).

This example was an experiment, but Stewart (1980) analysed the results of real-life juries in

Table 4.6: Summary of the results from Sigall and Ostrove (1975)

Average length of sentence in years

Crime	No photo	Attractive photo	Unattractive photo
Burglary	5.10	2.80	5.20
Fraud	4.35	5.45	4.35

Pennsylvania. Stewart rated the facial attractiveness of the defendants and the verdicts of the case. It was found that there was no correlation between facial attractiveness and perception of guilt. But for length of sentences, there was a negative correlation between reduced sentences and facial attractiveness for both sexes. Thus the more attractive the face, the shorter the sentence given when the defendant was found guilty.

Commentary

As a variation, Kerr (1978) has shown that the physical attractiveness of the victim can influence the verdict reached by the jury. In the experiment, mock jurors read about the theft of a car from a physically attractive or unattractive woman (with a photograph attached to the transcript). The physically attractive victim was more often supported with a guilty verdict, regardless of how much care she had taken to protect the vehicle (like using a steering lock or not).

Race
Again stereotypes are involved, but, in this case, there is evidence of racial bias. In a mock trial experiment, it was found that white students rated black defendants more guilty than white defendants, particularly when the victim was white (Pfeifer and Ogloff, 1991). Research on actual trials in USA found that black defendants received longer sentences than white defendants for the same offence (Stewart, 1980).

The OJ Simpson trial (1994/5) was viewed as a race-related trial by many. Stahly and Walker (1997), who worked for the legal defence team, noted the psychological processes at work among viewers of the trial. They highlighted group identity and the 'availability heuristic'. The availability heuristic is where we tend to recall only certain information when making a decision. For example, white Americans saw the obvious guilt of Simpson because of the physical evidence against him, while the African-Americans saw police misconduct.

Skolnick and Shaw (1997) used 213 students in a mock murder trial and varied the defendant's race and celebrity status. The former influenced the verdict, but not the latter (see Table 4.7, below).

Table 4.7: Summary of the results from Skolnick and Shaw (1997)

Juror's race	Defendant's race	Guilty verdict	Not guilty verdict
Black	Black	18.7%	32.7%
	White	33.6%	15.0%
White	Black	18.7%	29.2%
	White	22.6%	29.5%

Accent

Mahoney and Dixon (1997) report their research with the 'Brummie' (Birmingham) accent. Generally this accent is perceived of as low status. The researchers played a two-minute recording of a police interview with a suspect to 119 white non-Birmingham students. There were a number of versions of the recording played to different groups, including 'Brummie' accent versus 'non-Brummie', and white versus black 'Brummie'. The students had to assess whether they felt the speaker was guilty of a particular crime. The 'Brummie' accent was perceived as more guilty than the 'non-Brummie', and the black 'Brummie' was perceived as most guilty, particularly for 'blue-collar' crime (like theft).

Seggie (1983) found similar results in Australia. Using recordings of suspects arguing their innocence with either 'standard' ('received pronunciation': RP) or 'broad' Australian accents, or an 'Asian' accent, participants were asked to assess the level of guilt on particular crimes. The 'standard' accent was seen as most guilty on 'white-collar' crimes (like fraud), but the 'broad' accent was most guilty for 'blue-collar' crimes.

Miscellaneous

The following variables have all been found to influence the juror's decisions: 'powerful speech' (that is, speaking clearly and without hesitation) by the defendant, and their demeanour in court (for example, sitting up straight and paying attention to the evidence) (Hans and Vidmar, 1986). For example, during her trial in 1997, Louise Woodward (see page 61) showed no emotions, which the USA jury interpreted as a display of indifference. She was found guilty of 'second-degree murder' (Harrower, 1998).

Child witnesses

The general belief is that children under ten or eleven years of age are not trustworthy witnesses because of poor accuracy of recall, ease of suggestibility during interviews and because they are prone to fantasy. These traditional beliefs are often reinforced by legal textbooks.

Brown (1926) summarizes the traditional view: 'Create, if you will, an idea of what the child is to hear or see, and the child is very likely to hear or see what you desire' (quoted in Loftus, 1996). This belief remains even when the accuracy between the child and the adult witnesses is found to be the same in research.

Even the legal professionals hold similar views. Brigham and Spiers (1992) sent questionnaires to child protection workers, police officers and lawyers in Florida state. Their findings are summarized in Table 4.8 (see below).

Table 4.8: Summary of results from Brigham and Spiers (1992)

Comparison of 5–9 year olds with adults

	Defence	Prosecution	CPW*	Police
Likely to recall:				
* less/much less	96%	57%	55%	50%
* about same	4%	36%	30%	28%
* more/much more	0%	7%	14%	22%
Suggestible:				
* less/much less	1%	11%	20%	17%
* about same	3%	20%	13%	18%
* more/much more	96%	70%	67%	65%

* = chief prosecution witness

This refusal to trust children's testimonies is very important in child abuse cases. So it is necessary for psychology to try to establish the strengths and weaknesses of child witnesses. In other words, are the common sense beliefs about children's memories correct?

Accuracy of child witnesses

Generally, recall improves as the child gets older. For example, Ellis *et al* (1973) compared recall among a group of twelve and seventeen year olds. They were all shown 20 colour slides of faces of students, then four hours later had to pick them out from a collection of 60 slides. The seventeen year olds recalled an average of 79% of the faces, and the twelve year olds 72%.

However, young children can accurately recall information in familiar situations. Using free recall, children are worse than adults, but with verbal prompts (not leading questions) this can be improved.

Commentary

Recall is not the same for the whole situation. In other words, some aspects are better recalled than others. For example, in a general memory experiment, Fivush and Shukat (1995) report that three to five year olds are consistently better at recall of activities or objects than of people or locations.

Repeat interviewing

In many situations, the child is interviewed more than once. What is the effect of this on the accuracy of recall? Using a medical examination, Goodman and Schwartz-Kenney (1992) found that 'repeated interviews did not reduce the children's accuracy of report, and, if anything, actually improved it' (p. 21) for three to four and five to seven year olds. Those children interviewed twice were also less susceptible to misleading questions in the second interview.

KEY STUDY 8

Researchers:	Brown, Salmon and Pipe *et al* (1999)
Aim:	To assess the accuracy of recall of a real medical examination that is painful and stressful to the child.
Method:	Twenty children between three and five years old were undergoing actual medical examinations in New Zealand. The children were either undergoing an internal X-ray of their kidneys (known as 'voiding cysto-urethrogram' – VCUG), which is very painful, or a general examination (pediatric assessment – PA).
Results:	The VCUG group remembered more of what happened six to eight days later, but at the expense of accuracy. Mean correct recall of actions was 6.70 (out of 28) for the VCUG group, and 4.10 for PA group, while mean total errors were 0.8 and 0.3 respectively.
Conclusions:	Pain and stress were shown to affect recall negatively.

Most of the research is experimental, based on artificial situations. But Key Study 8 is an example of research in a real life situation. Overall, like adults, children remember the essential facts of important events accurately, and they give false reports only when trying to hide something.

Suggestibility of child witnesses

Since 1979, there have been over 100 studies on the suggestibility of child witnesses. There are two key questions that emerge from the research.

- Are children more suggestible than adults?
- Under what conditions are children's statements distorted?

Children are always interviewed by an adult who is more powerful than them. Children tend to want to please and to assume that the adult knows anyway, or knows best. For example, Peters (1987) found that children would more often pick a photo from a selection to identify a person seen at the dentist, even when the actual person's photo was not included. It is very hard for the child to question the adult's authority and say the photo is not there. When the photo was included, accuracy was around 30% correct.

Roberts and Lamb (1999) looked at how often children correct distortions made by the adult interviewer in real-life abuse cases in the USA. They discovered 140 distortions in 68 formal interviews with three to fourteen year olds. An example of a distortion would be the child saying 'by the school', and the interviewer later saying 'inside the school'. The children corrected the distortions one-third of the time, but only when the distortions were not complex.

However, giving children pre-interview training with practice questions can reduce the impact of misleading questions, without reducing the accuracy of the information.

Commentary

Children are particularly prone to conformity. So if they hear other children (seven to thirteen year olds) giving answers, they will copy them – even if the information is wrong. Children who are told something is a secret are less willing to tell.

Misleading questions do influence the answers children give, but such questions also affect adult witnesses. Warning beforehand about such questions is helpful for both groups.

Fantasy/reality

It has often been suggested that children make up stories about abuse. For example, Taylor in 1849 estimated the figure to be 93%, and Brouardel in 1907, 60%–80% (both quoted in Spencer and Flin, 1993). But in a more recent survey of nearly 600 cases of sexual abuse, less than 10% were found to be fictitious and many of these fictions had been created by adults, not the children initially (King and Yuille, 1987).

Experimentally, Saywitz et al (1991) have tested how children respond to genital touch. During a medical examination of 72 five to seven year old girls, half received a genital examination. This latter group tended not to report the genital touch in free recall one week later, but only when asked a leading question. For the other group, who didn't receive a genital examination, none falsely reported having been touched in free recall. However, three children did give false reports to leading questions.

Generally, children's reports can be assessed using techniques like 'statement validity analysis'. This can be used for all witness statements by looking for underlying criteria. In other words, it would have to be a very complex fabrication by the child to not be recognized by this technique.

Special circumstances

Dent (1992) arranged for an incident to happen in the classrooms of three groups of participants:

- 78 eight to twelve year old children with learning difficulties
- 102 children aged nine to ten without learning difficulties
- 65 adults.

All the groups were interviewed one week later, and all were equally accurate in free recall and in answer to general questions. However, the children with learning difficulties were poorest with specific questions. There was no difference between the adult witnesses and the children without learning difficulties on specific questions. The key was the method used to interview the witnesses.

Conclusions

Tavris and Wade (1995) draw the following conclusions about child witnesses.

- They can be influenced by misleading questions, like adults. Pre-school children are most vulnerable.

- They are influenced by stereotypes in their recall, like adults.
- They usually know reality from fantasy, but this may blur in emotionally intense situations.
- The answers given to adults may be what is expected (or what the child thinks is expected).
- The emotional tone of the interview can influence the accuracy of recall – for example, questioning under pressure leads to inaccuracies. But, again, this is true of adults.

Effects of testifying on child witnesses

The trauma for a child giving evidence in court and being cross-examined makes it even more difficult to use children's evidence to convict. In fact, a number of abuse cases have collapsed because of the child's inability to cope in court. Cross-examination in court is even difficult for adults.

Goodman et al (1992) noticed that 20 out of 40 US children they formally observed showed signs of distress at the preliminary hearings, and 11 out of 17 showed distress during the trial.

The whole criminal justice system is complex and incomprehensible for many adults, let alone children. These children can be affected at different stages of the procedure (see Table 4.9 below, and 4.10, p. 71).

Table 4.9: Factors in the trial process causing children stress

Pre-trial	Trial	Post-trial
Repeated interviews	Waiting in court	No debriefing or follow-up
Lack of understanding of legal terms and so on	Lack of knowledge of legal procedure	Unsuccessful prosecution
Waiting for trial (without counselling)	Layout and size of courtroom	
Rescheduling of trial	Giving evidence and cross-examination	
Removal of child from home	Confronting accused	
Retaliation		
Fear of unknown		
Media reporting		

Improving trial procedures to help child witnesses

There are a number of ways this can be done, as the text that follows explains.

Table 4.10: Effects of stress of the trial on the child

Mediating factors:	Crime:	Pre-trial:	Trial:	Post-trial:
• conduct of trial	• post-traumatic effects	• anxiety	• anxiety	• behavioural difficulties (negative)
• preparation		• apprehension	• excitement	• relief (positive) depending on verdict
• social support		• sleep, appetite and mood changes	• tension	
• family reaction			• fear	
• age			• crying	
• personality			• disruption of cognitive and communication skills	

Source: Spencer and Flin, 1993.

Interviewing the child witness

It is important that children are interviewed by adults who have no prior knowledge of what happened, and to try and explain this to the child. One technique uses a game involving a child's head and an adult's head. The adult's head is empty and the child's is full of counters to show that the child has the knowledge. As the child recounts the events, he/she places the counters in the adult's head. Using this technique, children gave longer accounts relative to an interview that didn't use this game (Poole, 1992; quoted in Harrower, 1998).

Since the Criminal Justice Act (1991), the videoing of the first interview with the child can be used as evidence in court. The interview is usually conducted in line with the 'Memorandum of Good

Table 4.11: Recommendations for video-recorded interviews with children

Phase	Approach	Avoid
1 Rapport	Relax child	Mentioning offence
2 Free narrative account	Allow child to talk about offence (Adult mainly listening)	Direct questions (adult speaking too much)
3 Questioning:		
a open-ended questions	General then specific questions, non-leading	Repeating questions and complex ones
b specific yet non-leading questions	Specific questions	Forced choice questions
c closed questions	Forced choice questions	Questions that require same answer
d leading questions	Questions about disputed facts	
4 Closing the interview	'Rapport' and thank child	Summary in adult language

Source: Home Office, 1992.

Table 4.12: Examples of considerations for talking to young children

Avoid	Use
Long complex sentences	Short sentences
Three or four syllable words	One or two syllable words
Multi-verb words (for example, 'might have been')	Simple tenses (for example, '-ed', 'was')
Pronouns	Proper nouns
Relational terms (for example, 'more', 'less')	Concrete visualizable terms (for example, 'a lot', 'a little')
Uncommon negatives (for example, 'Is that not true?')	Positive constructions (for example, 'Is that true?')
Hypotheticals (for example, 'If you want a break, then let me know')	Direct approach (for example, 'Are you tired?' 'Do you want a break?')

Source: Saywitz, 1995.

Practice on Video Recorded Interviews with Child Witnesses for Criminal Proceedings' (1992) produced by the Home Office. 'The questioning by the police officer or social worker, in effect, replaces examination of the child by an advocate in court' (p. 2).

The interviewer is encouraged to establish rapport with the child, use open-ended questions and allow free recall time, then finish the interview with reassurance. The length should be no more than one hour. The interviewer is also restricted because of the need to produce good legal evidence, and must wait for the child to give the name or the offence before using any leading questions (see Tables 4.11 and 4.12, on this page).

The main advantage of this type of video interview is that it can preserve the accuracy of the recall without multiple interviews, and the child can use his/her own words. But the defendant loses the right to cross-examine this evidence. Concern has been voiced that it is harder to detect if children are lying on video. Westcott *et al* (1991) found only 59% accuracy by adult jurors in telling if a child on a video had been on a museum trip or not. However, individuals are generally poorer at detecting deception than is usually thought.

In practice, however, only a few video interviews are used in court; approximately 5% in 1992/3 (Social Services Inspectorate, 1994). This works out at around 130 videotaped interviews by each police authority, with only seven of them being used in court.

Commentary

Initial research has found no difference in the number of guilty verdicts between trials with video evidence and live witnesses (Davies *et al*, 1995)

Children giving evidence

The Criminal Justice Act (1988) allowed for children to testify in court by closed-circuit television ('live link') in England and Wales. The room used is next to the courtroom, and the interaction between the lawyers and the child can be controlled by the judge.

Davies and Noon (1991) have studied its use in England and Wales. Compared to children in open court, the 'live link' children cried less, were less unhappy, could give more consistent answers, and were more resistant to leading questions. It is thought to be less traumatic for the child also. But there is concern about the loss of the rights of the defendant in this situation. Murray (1995) studying the use of 'live link' in Scotland found the children produced poorer quality evidence.

One area of development is in preparing the child for the court visit. Overall special programmes do improve the child's ability to testify, and reduce the anxiety involved (see Table 4.13, next column). In the UK, West Yorkshire Police piloted such a programme, but it was never fully implemented (Satter, 1998). The NSPCC does produce 'The Child Witness Pack'.

Offender punishment and rehabilitation

With regards the type and role of punishment, this will depend on the theory held for the cause of crime. If the cause is 'dispositional' (that is, something wrong with the criminal), then it is necessary

Table 4.13: Programmes to help prepare children for giving evidence in court

London Family Court Clinic, Ontario, Canada: child witness project	National Children's Advocacy Centre, USA
Courtroom model and doll	Session 1: artwork about court
Specialized booklets	Session 2: role-play court activities
Role-playing and dressing up in courtroom clothes	Session 3: tour of empty courthouse
Homework	Sessions 4/5: role-play in empty courtroom
Court tour	Session 6: overview/ 'graduation certificate'
Stress-reduction techniques	
Source: Dezwirek-Sas, 1992.	Source: Sisterman *et al*, 1992.

to change that disposition. This is where treatment for offenders comes in, and the aim is to rehabilitate the offender. Rehabilitation can be defined as 'the result of any planned interaction that reduces an offender's further criminal activity, whether that is mediated by personality, behaviour, abilities, attitudes, values or other factors' (The Panel on Research in Rehabilitative Techniques quoted in Blackburn, 1993).

Commentary

Carroll *et al* (1987) in a survey of attitudes towards sentencing found two broad approaches: 'conservative' and 'liberal'. The first approach is in favour of punishment because criminals have chosen that career, and need to be discouraged from it in some way. The latter sees the need to rehabilitate the offender.

Secure institutions: prisons

The theory behind the use of prison is three-fold: to act as a deterrent, to protect the general public, and to provide rehabilitation for the offender.

In attempting to stop recidivism, a variety of approaches have been taken in UK prisons. One approach is the 'short, sharp shock' regime for young offenders, which attempts to 'shock' them from committing future crimes, by a highly unpleasant custodial sentence. It involves strict discipline, kit inspection, drill, brisk routines, extended physical exercise and close supervision. It is a political decision to introduce such regimes, because research finds no difference between this method and an ordinary prison in stopping re-offending (for example, Thornton *et al*, 1984).

Commentary

In fact, interviews with some young offenders showed that they preferred this technique because it helped to pass the time and they enjoyed the physical exercise. It must be remembered that what one person finds aversive, another does not.

The psychotherapeutic unit

The complete alternative is the idea of a psychotherapeutic unit, such as Grendon Prison in Scotland. This involves focusing the whole institution on therapy, and finding the reasons for the offending behaviour. Unfortunately, this approach has proved no more successful in stopping re-offending behaviour either (Gunn and Robertson, 1982). But is the role of prison to 'cure' criminal behaviour?

Any attempt at rehabilitation in prison is hampered by 'criminalization' and 'prisonization'. With 'criminalization', inmates share their views and create a joint 'deviant sub-culture' with their own loyalties and commitments. The latter process is the learning of the appropriate formal and informal rules for the prison sub-culture, which again is in conflict with general society. Thus the 'more time one spends in prison, the more likely one is to re-offend' (Bartol, 1999).

Within the prison, there will be the institutional needs (including security and management) and the inmates' needs. Both sets of needs are intertwined (for example, a badly-managed prison affects the inmates).

The experience of prison

In a mock jail experiment (the Stanford Prison Simulation), Haney *et al* (1973) found that both prisoners and prison officers took on the role expectations of the institution. This made the prison officers aggressive and controlling, and the prisoners depressed. This study emphasized how the environment influences/controls behaviour. But it was only a mock jail with student volunteers.

The psychological effect of imprisonment varies from individual to individual, though for many it has a strong negative effect. Research in North America tends to find initial psychological problems at the beginning of the sentence, and after the inmate has adjusted, no long term emotional problems. Problems may reappear towards the end of the sentence. However, prisoners find ways of surviving psychologically (see RLA 14, next column).

Real Life Application 14: Banged up

Bruce Jones interviewed a number of inmates, former inmates and prison officers from British jails for the BBC Radio 5 series *Laying Down the Law*. The picture they all paint is very negative. Here are some of the main points made.

- Cruelty and aggression by prisoners and prison officers is common.
- Prisoners wish their lives away.
- Prisoners feel of abandoned, that nobody cares, and that there is no sympathy for them.
- Prisoners attempt to fill the day with something, like a hobby (for example, one prisoner designed a house using prices of materials from trade catalogues and building regulations given to him by prison officers).
- Tiny things become important, and any change can lead to unrest (for example, at one prison the cooks changed fish and chips from Fridays to Tuesday, which caused a prison riot).
- 'Jail sex' is rife – that is, heterosexual men using other prisoners. 'They would never think of themselves as homosexual,' said one prisoner.

Source: *Laying Down the Law*: 'Banged Up', 1995.

Summary

- The experience of prison is psychologically very negative, and prisoners have to make cognitive changes to cope.

Questions

1 Why do 'tiny things matter' in prison?
2 Research shows that psychological problems can reappear just before release from prison. Why might this happen?
3 Why is 'jail sex' an example of the psychological coping mechanism of denial?

Severe effects of imprisonment

For a small number of offenders, the experience of imprisonment is too much and they commit suicide, attempt it unsuccessfully (parasuicide), or engage in deliberate self-harm (DSH). In the most extensive historical study in the UK, Topp (1979) estimated the suicide rate for prisoners serving longer than eighteen months as 65 per 100,000. This is much higher than the figure for the general population. For males generally it is 16 per 100,000 people, and five for females (Zimbardo *et al*, 1995).

Inch, Rowlands and Soliman (1995) showed that being bullied and being locked up for long periods in a cell were the main reasons behind DSH at a young offenders' institution in northern England. DSH may involve cutting the body or swallowing sharp objects. It is not necessarily parasuicide. Previous psychiatric treatment was a key predictor of who harmed themselves.

However, many prisons are overcrowded and this can have specific effects on the inmates. Overcrowding has been linked to physical illness, socially disruptive behaviour, and emotional distress.

Paulus (1988) undertook a fifteen-year project on prison crowding. There was a direct relationship between the number of inmates in each housing unit and negative psychological (for example, anxiety and depression), and physical problems (for example, headaches and high blood pressure). The key is the number of residents sharing the space, not the space available. Providing privacy with screens, for example, reduced the negative impact of living in a large dormitory.

Paulus also found that the experience of jail was mediated by certain variables. High socio-economic status and educational level led to more difficulty in tolerating crowding, and prior prison confinement in individual cells also had similar problems. The effect of crowding is through a loss of control, the inability to achieve personal goals and the excessive stimulation of others. The other extreme to this situation is prisoners in isolation, either as punishment or for their own protection. The response to such a situation varies between individuals, but most people can endure short periods (like a few days).

Residential settings

These are institutions that are less concerned with security and more with treatment.

Therapeutic communities

The aim in this type of community is less with punishment and more about confronting the causes of the criminal behaviour. Unfortunately, UK research has found no difference in their reduction of recidivism for thirteen to fifteen year olds, compared to 'Approved schools' (Cornish and Clarke, 1975). Similarly, Jesness (1975), in the USA, found no difference in recidivism between therapeutic communities based on transactional analysis or behaviour modification techniques.

Community programmes

These are a set of programmes that attempt to tackle offending behaviour at a family or community level, or by discouraging criminal behaviour in the first place.

Individual and group therapy

In the American Cambridge-Somerville Youth Study, started in 1939, young males in high delinquency areas were assigned counsellors, given academic teaching, medical and psychiatric care and other community assistance. The programme lasted up to eight years. Research finds that again this project does not reduce future offending. However, many problems were created by the counsellors imposing social values which produced conflict for the participants and their families (McCord, 1978).

Commentary

Generally, family therapy as a treatment has become more popular in an attempt to reduce delinquency. There is Parent Management Training (PMT), which focuses on training the parental skills to deal with problem behaviour, while Functional Family Therapy (FFT) concentrates on the interactive process within the family system. Alexander and Parsons (1973) found lower recidivism in an eighteenth month follow-up, when comparing a FFT group with a control group (that is, no family therapy). The pitfall is with family therapy is that the family often gets the blame as the cause of crime.

Probation

Probation officers have traditionally been encouraged to develop behaviour programmes for their clients.

An important variable here is 'personally meaningful employment' during or after the probation and after release from an institution. Individuals engaged in rewarding employment are less likely to offend or re-offend. In other words, the rewards of the job (that is, financial and personal) are greater than those of crime. Unemployment among ex-offenders is much higher than the average, and the recidivism rate for the unemployed is four times greater than for the employed ex-offender.

Divisionary projects

The kind of projects involved include reparation, community centres, and intermediate treatment

(IT). The last two projects attempt to prevent offending, while the first is a form of punishment.

An example of IT in the UK is Salamanca House (Lambeth) set up to contact and work with 'unclubbable' youngsters in the area. In the two years after it was set up in 1973, there were two new youth clubs, street-based adventure and sporting activities, and two education and training schemes (Preston, 1982).

In America, Davidson *et al* (1987) found that juvenile offenders on divisionary projects had fewer future court appearances than a control group not on any programme. But on a measure of self-reported delinquency, there was no difference.

Attempts have been made in the UK to use diversion as an alternative to prison for offenders with mental health problems. It is aimed at breaking the cycle of offending, imprisonment and re-offending among a vulnerable group. The diversion options available under the Mental Health Act 1983 include remand to a psychiatric hospital or a probation order with the condition of outpatient psychiatric treatment (Gibson, 1997).

Psychological techniques used in the treatment of offenders

There are a number of these, which are covered in the text that follows.

Behaviour modification

These techniques have been adapted into the 'Token Economy System' (TES). The individual gains points or tokens for 'good behaviour', and loses them for 'bad behaviour'. After a while, the tokens gained can be exchanged for desirable activities (like watching TV) or objects (like cigarettes).

The TES has been implemented in whole prisons in the USA (for example, 'Cell Block Token Economy' Milan *et al*, 1974). In the UK, there has been limited use in 'Young Offenders Institutions' (for example, Cullen and Seddon, 1981).

At Camp Butner, North Carolina, aluminium tokens were used with the inmates. For example, fighting lead to 'seclusion', a charge of fifteen tokens, with inmates sent their rooms to be quiet for 30 minutes. If they fulfilled this criteria, they received five tokens.

Commentary

On the whole these programmes are successful in controlling offences within the institution and during the programme. But the real success is whether any behaviour changes continue outside the institution and after the programme stops. Unfortunately, the ability of TES to stop recidivism is weak.

Other problems include the creation of a mercenary attitude, or that some inmates who are unable to control their behaviour, receive no tokens and experience learned helplessness. This is the feeling that the individual has no control over events, and they tend to be passive to life's challenges. These feelings can easily lead the offender into the old cycle of behaviour and recidivism. Other techniques based on behaviourist principles have been tried. For example, reparation programmes require the offender to make a personal apology and/or financial compensation to the victim. This is uncomfortable, and acts as punishment to stop future offending.

Social skills training

One approach to help the offenders is by giving them social skills training (SST). It is hoped that this will give them an alternative to violence or crime. It can also be a way of improving the individual's employment skills.

SST does change the social behaviour of participants, but it may not necessarily prevent crime or re-offending behaviour. Spence and Marziller (1979) worked with five male young offenders who had few close friends, and were aggressive and rude. Videos of their behaviour showed they avoided eye contact, made inappropriate head movements, had excessive hand fiddlings, gave few verbal acknowledgements and a lack of feedback. Each participant received seven to ten training sessions using modelling, role-playing, videotaped feedback and social reinforcement. The results were increased eye contact and reduced hand fiddling, but no change otherwise. This is because of problems with maintaining and generalizing changes in skills, the poor motivation of some individuals to change, and even institutional resistance in some prisons (Howells, 1986).

Cognitive behavioural therapy (CBT)

This technique is based on the assumption that thoughts are the basis of behaviour, and a change in thinking patterns will change the behaviour. So, for example, attempts are made to encourage different attributions about others (that is, not hostile or aggressive). This can be achieved by self-instructional training, modelling or role-playing.

Self-instructional training focuses on the self-statements individuals use and how to modify them to achieve self-control. It may involve being less critical and making more positive self-statements. Studies have found that it does increase self-control (and consequently reduces aggressive behaviour) among young offenders.

Concerning role-taking, Chandler (1973) developed a programme for young offenders that involved taking the perspective of the victim. In an eighteen month follow-up, those offenders from the programme had committed significantly fewer offences than a control group.

Other cognitive behavioural type programmes include social problem-solving, and moral reasoning development. Social problem-solving teaches offenders cognitive skills like sensitivity to interpersonal problems, consequential thinking and alternative strategies. Moral reasoning development involves offenders discussing and justifying moral decisions. This was shown to improve moral development.

Anger control programmes

The original idea for these programmes comes from Raymond Novaco (1975), who emphasized the role of cognitions in anger (that is, thoughts that precede anger or aggression). This is very similar to the ideas behind CBT. The expression of the anger becomes reinforcing and a pattern is set for future behaviour. But anger is not necessarily all bad; it is a question of managing it, and self-control.

Anger control programmes tend to be based on three stages.

- Cognitive preparation – careful analysis of anger patterns allows the individual to recognize his/her own patterns – in particular to identify triggers, then to follow the process.
- Skill acquisition – this stage involves the teaching of techniques to use when the triggers for anger come. This could include self-awareness that an anger-provoking situation is developing and using self-talk to stop the aggressive reaction. Other skills could include relaxation training, assertiveness training and social skills training.
- Application practice – this last stage involves creating stressful situations that provoke anger, so that the newly learned techniques can be applied. There is then an assessment of how the situation was handled by the individual themselves and the therapist.

McDougall *et al* (1987) studied eighteen young offenders in prison who went through a course of anger control and found it reduced offences in prison by these individuals.

Commentary: Controlling aggression – reward or punishment

- Punishment of aggressive behaviour – generally punishment of aggressive behaviour has some effect, but it can lead to displaced aggression elsewhere. Sherman and Berk (1984) found that arresting the violent partner in domestic violence cases was most effective by the Minneapolis police department. There were only 10% cases of re-offending compared to 24% for 'separating partners for cooling down period' or 19% for 'counselling both parties'.
- Punishment of aggressive models – Bandura's work on observational learning and modelling has shown that seeing an aggressive model being punished reduces overt aggression (Bandura, Ross and Ross, 1963). But it does not produce long-term change as the aggressive behaviour will appear if rewards are offered later for such behaviour.
- Rewarding alternative behaviour patterns – it is better to reward non-aggressive behaviour patterns. Brown and Elliot (1965) asked nursery school teachers to ignore aggressive behaviour among the children and give attention only when desired behaviour was shown. The average number of aggressive acts fell from 64 before the experiment to 26 two weeks later.

Psychodynamic therapy

Psychodynamic therapy is based on the work of Sigmund Freud. The aim is to discover the childhood and/or unconscious cause of the behaviour. This tends to have limited use because it is time-consuming and can be superficial, if not handled correctly.

Persons (1967) performed one of the few outcome studies on its use with boys at a reform school. The 82 boys were matched on demographic and criminal variables, and half were randomly chosen to receive 80 hours of therapy over 20 weeks. The therapy was individual psychoanalysis or 'eclectic' (combination of approaches) group therapy. Immediately afterwards, 30 of the treatment group showed less psychological problems compared to 12 in the control group, while one year later, 13 of the treated and 25 of the untreated boys had been re-institutionalized. Generally the treated group did better, but the improvement could either be due to the therapy or, alternatively, due to the attention given to the boys in the treatment group.

Humanistic approaches

Therapies here tend to concentrate on self-awareness, the present, personal growth and the exercise of autonomy. This type of approach is rarely used because again it can be time-consuming. However, Jesness (1975) compared its use in California with adolescent offenders in similar institutions using the Token Economy System. The use of humanistic therapy produced greater attitude changes, but less change in overt behaviour. There was no difference in parole violation one year later between the two techniques. However, both techniques produced better results than those in similar institutions without either.

What works?

It seems that most outcome studies find little success in reducing recidivism, whatever the technique used. But many studies have methodological weaknesses or are too general in the approaches to recidivism.

Based on 231 studies, Martinson (1974) is best known for concluding that 'nothing works'. But Thornton (1987) re-analysed the same data using a clear definition of recidivism and controls in the allocation of groups for the studies. On this basis, only 34 of the studies were acceptable in comparing psychological therapies to an untreated control group. Of the 34, 16 showed a significant benefit from treatment, 17 showed no difference and only one study found a significant disadvantage following treatment. This has led to the current position that 'clinical intervention works with some offenders, some of the time' (Hollin, 1989). This is known as 'differential treatment'.

Recent research has involved meta-analysis (a sophisticated statistical technique) to compare other studies. For example, Losel (1995) summarized the meta-analysis of 500+ studies on the effect of correctional treatment since the mid-1980s. The mean effect size was 0.10 (which means a 10% drop in recidivism due to treatment).

Overall, for treatments to reduce recidivism the programme needs to follow certain criteria.

- Application of a specific structure to a specific problem (for example, Behaviour Therapy for aggression).
- The staff need to model and reinforce anti-criminal values.
- The staff need to be committed to the programme.
- Attitudes that encourage offending behaviour must be challenged.
- The programme must be matched to the offender.
- These should be an attempt to generalize the programme outside of the institution.

Hollin (1992) draws some conclusions about therapeutic programmes, as listed below.

- Multi-modal structured treatments are effective. For example, Aggression Replacement Training (ART) uses three main approaches: structured learning training (including social skills training and social problem-solving), anger control training, and moral education. In a New York study, re-arrest rates for those on ART were 15% compared to 43% for the control group (Goldstein *et al*, 1989). Lipsey's (1992) meta-analysis of 400 studies of juvenile delinquency found a reduction in recidivism of around 20% for skill-oriented, CBT, and multi-modal programmes.
- Behavioural-based approaches are much better than psychotherapy.
- Community programmes and those involving the family are also effective.

On the other hand, there are threats to such programmes, such as: 'programme drift' (a move from the original aims of the programme), 'programme reversal' (staff modelling inappropriate behaviour), and 'programme non-compliance' (the programme changing half-way through) (Hollin, 1995).

Reducing the opportunities for crime

The text that follows examines how hardening the target and removing the target may help in reducing the opportunities for crime.

Hardening the target

This involves making the target physically difficult to break into, like the many changes in car design. Mayhew *et al* (1976) showed that the compulsory fitting of steering column locks to cars in West Germany in the 1960s led to a 60% drop in car theft.

Practically individual houses can be hardened against burglars with good locks, door chains, high gates, alarms and security lights (see Table 4.14, page 78). Target hardening, however, can be expensive.

Removing the target

This is the removal of the potential targets of crime. For example, the payment of salaries by bank account reduces the number of security vans carrying large sums of cash.

During the 1960s and 1970s, British Gas was detoxified (that is, it is no longer lethal) and consequently the suicide rate has declined. So if people could not 'gas themselves', then there was no displacement to other methods of suicide.

Commentary

In West Germany, by 1980 it was compulsory for motor-cyclists to wear helmets, and this was seen as reducing motor-cycle theft by 60% between 1980 and 1986.

Table 4.14: 1996 British Crime Survey
Points of entry by burglars

Door	66%
(backdoor	50%)

Proportion of entry not gained because of:

door locks	45%
sensor lights	45%
window locks	46%
door chain	47%
dog	52%
burglar alarm	62%
3+ of measures	52%

Unless an offender was carrying his/her own motorcycle helmet, opportunist crime was very limited.

Increasing the risk of detection

Increasing the risk of detection can be undertaken by formal surveillance and informal surveillance, as the text that follows explains.

Formal surveillance

This involves 'authority figures' in different ways: police patrols reduce general levels of crime, bus conductors reduce vandalism of the bus, shop assistants reduce shoplifting, door attendants in apartment blocks reduce burglary.

A common sight now in public places is closed circuit television (CCTV). When this was first introduced to the London Underground in the late 1970s, it reduced crime on certain stations by 70%. Before CCTV, there were 252 offences reported on the four stations studied compared to 75 after the installation (Burrows, 1980). However, there was evidence of 'displacement' to the nearby stations that did not have CCTV.

The introduction of CCTV in town centres has also reduced crime – for example, there was a reduction of 27% in Northampton after the introduction of 120 cameras in 1993 (Harrower, 1998).

Commentary

In a campaign to enforce driving speed limits in the Netherlands, increased surveillance by the police reduced speeding, but did not produce a change in attitudes towards speeding.

Informal surveillance

This technique involves encouraging the public reporting of crime. The best known scheme is the 'Neighbourhood Watch'. The principle behind this scheme is that people living in the same area will watch out for each other's property. It is not clear whether such schemes do reduce crime, but it does increase security awareness and reporting to the police.

Crime prevention programmes

Welsh and Farrington (1999) reviewed the studies on crime prevention programmes. Two examples proved to be particularly successful. First was the Seattle Community Crime Prevention Programme launched in 1973. Advice was given to householders to avoid burglary as well as public information about crime. It included property marking and neighbourhood watch schemes. There was a 61% drop in crime after one year, with no evidence of territorial displacement.

In the UK, there was the Kirkholt Burglary Prevention Project (Rochdale) between March 1987 and February 1990. This included the marking of property, 'target hardening' (the reduction of vulnerable points of entrance to the house like windows without locks), neighbourhood watch, and 'target removal' (for example, the removal of coin gas and electricity meters). Over the three years of the project, reported burglaries fell from 526 per annum to 132 (a reduction of 75%).

This links with the work of Newman (1972) on 'defensible space'. He noted that New York apartment blocks that had areas of public territory (like lifts, stairs or foyers) which didn't belong to individual tenants, suffered more vandalism and crime. In other words, where the blocks felt like an individual's territory, this reduced crime. Newman drew out four factors to make an area 'defensible space'.

- Territory – make every part of the building feel like somebody's territory (for example, individual entrances to flats are better than large entrances for many flats).
- Surveillance – make all areas observable. Research has shown that public telephones that are observable from houses or flats receive less vandalism than those hidden from view.
- Image – buildings that look secure stop opportunistic crime.
- Milieu – apply the same principles to the area around the housing (for example, not having lots of bushes nearby).

Wilson (1980) compared housing blocks in inner London and, in particular, entrance design. If the entrance acted as routes to other locations there was more vandalism than if the entrance was solely for the residents.

Commentary

Other research has shown that design changes by themselves could not produce long-term reductions in crime. For example, design changes (like removing overhead walkways) on the Mozart Estate (London) cut burglaries, assaults and street robberies for five months, but then they rose again (quoted in Hall, 1995).

Designing crime out

The idea of 'designing crime out' has developed and become more common. Burglars, for example, can be discouraged by barriers (for example, fences and walls – not necessarily very high), and markers (that is, signs that the territory is inhabited, like house name plates).

Personal skills

Another approach to preventing crime is to change the potential victim. In other words, potential victims are made more aware of the risks, and given strategies to deal with those risks. This approach has been applied in the UK in, for example, government booklets like 'Practical Ways to Crack Crime'. Recommendations include avoiding isolated bus stops at night, not stopping for hitch-hikers when driving alone, and not parking in a dimly-lit area.

Most of the advice is aimed at women and what they can do to protect themselves from crime. But Stanko (1990), argues from a feminist perspective that this type of advice raises fears rather than lessens them. In fact, by placing the burden of safety on women's shoulders, it is 'formulating a new version of blaming women for their victimization' (p. 179). Furthermore, Stanko argues that this type of advice ignores the danger of violence from known men. Statistically, rape is more likely to be committed by someone known to the victim rather than a complete stranger.

Personal skills can also be applied to children in relation to sexual abuse. These include encouraging children to be assertive when being touched in an unpleasant way and the concept of body ownership.

Zero tolerance

This concept has developed recently, particularly in American cities, and involves a police crackdown on any and every crime. The assumption is that stopping small crimes will also reduce bigger ones.

Alternatively, letting the small crimes go unpunished leads to disorder and bigger crimes. The original idea was formulated in 1982 in an article called 'Broken Windows' in the *Atlantic Monthly* magazine by James Wilson and George Kelling. For example, the presence of graffiti leads to the belief, so the argument goes, that people do not care for the neighbourhood and there are few inhibitions to further crime.

In New York, zero tolerance was introduced in 1992 and produced a 25% increase in arrests, but a reduction in serious crimes. The number of homicides fell from 2,166 in 1991 to 767 in 1997.

Why does such a policy reduce serious crime? It is probably a combination of factors – increased police effort and resources are available, and an increased number of offenders locked away. In fact, part of New York's success is due to an extra 7,000 police officers introduced with the zero tolerance policy in a city that already had a high ratio of police to public.

Bowling (1999) argues that part of the success in reducing homicides was due to the decline in the 'crack market', which had peaked in the mid-1990s. He also argued that the politicians claimed responsibility for the success of zero tolerance and ignored the community crime preventions organized by ordinary New Yorkers, like citizen patrols or shopping escorts for older people.

In the UK, a number of local authorities have attempted to introduce zero tolerance policies, for example, on domestic violence. Edinburgh City Council attempted to raise awareness of domestic violence, rape and child sexual abuse through media campaigns. Meanwhile, in Chester, attempts were made to dispel the common myths of 'stranger danger' with adverts, posters and exhibitions on violence against women and children.

Essay questions

1 Discuss the factors involved in jury decision making.
2 What is recidivism? Describe and evaluate the different methods of punishment and rehabilitation that are used to try and reduce recidivism.
3 Compare and contrast tertiary crime prevention with environmental crime prevention.

 # Advice on answering essay questions

Chapter 1

1 Answers should describe the three most commonly used methods (police statistics, victim surveys, and offender surveys). The better answers will then compare each of the methods showing their strengths and weaknesses. Thus no method by itself gives a complete picture of the amount of crime.

2 This question is about weighing up the nature and nurture debate on the personality of police officers. The nature side argues for a certain type of person who becomes a police officer (that is, the 'police personality'), while the nurture side proposes that the police sub-culture changes different personality types to fit into a standard 'police personality'.

3 The question is looking for the different types of false confession, and some of the reasons for false confessions. The reasons may be within the individual (for example, need for social approval) or within the context of the police interview (for example, police control of the situation).

Chapter 2

1 This is a nature/nurture question for criminal behaviour. The nature side argues that certain people are born to become criminals because of, for example, genes or neurological damage, while the nurture side believes that anybody can become a criminal, it depends on their environment. The best answers will highlight the methodological problems of both these approaches.

2 There are a number of differences in thinking patterns between criminals and non-criminals (for example, as noted in the work of Yochelson and Samenow). These includes attributions like the 'Hostile Attribution Bias'. But there are also cases where criminals do not think differently – for example, rapist and non-rapist men's attitudes to 'date rape'.

3 The main difference between these two approaches revolves around how data is collected. The British approach tends to look for statistical patterns in certain types of crimes (for example, Canter's work on rapists). The American approach revolves around in-depth interviews with, for example, serial killers in prison.

Chapter 3

1 This question is asking for a survey of the factors that influence eye-witness memory (like post-event leading questions). The best answers will point out that most of the traditional research is from artificial experiments.

2 The best methods used by the police are those based on psychological principles – for example, cognitive interviews or returning to the scene of the event. The main principle is to help the witness find cues to aid recall.

3 The British Crime Survey is an example of a victim survey. What these surveys show is that a large amount of crime goes unreported to the police or is not included in official statistics. It also shows the reasons why people do not report crimes.

Chapter 4

1 This question involves looking at the three groups of factors that influence the juries beyond the actual evidence. These are trial influences (for example, small group decision-making processes), perceptions of the witnesses and the defendant (for example, of physical appearance), and the arguments of lawyers to persuade the jury.

2 Recidivism is when offenders commit further crimes after release from prison. There are a number of different institutions available for offenders – from prisons for punishment to rehabilitative communities. The success of each one depends on many factors like the type of crime, or the amount of support after release.

3 Tertiary crime prevention is the provision of treatment rather than punishment for offenders. This may include some type of therapy and is applied after the crime has been committed. Environmental crime prevention attempts to change the environment to stop crime occurring in the first place.

A Advice on answering short answer questions

RLA 1

1 Pearse and Gudjonsson (1999) found that interviews involving intimidation and manipulation are often classed as inadmissible in court.

2 Over 730.

3 Assertive interviewees who are confident of their rights or their innocence; silent interviewees who refuse to answer the questions.

RLA 2

1 Because the research findings are divided about the effectiveness of polygraphs, it is seen as better to watch the suspect closely instead.

2 Generally listening to what people say gives more clues to whether they are lying or not. In time people will often say something that can be proved to be a lie.

3 A polygraph is a device used to measure the autonomic nervous system (for example, heart rate, breathing rate), and it is used by some to detect liars.

RLA 3

1 She was worried that other people would be wondering where she was. This added to the pressure of the situation.

2 Her state of mind; the police control of the situation.

3 Coerced-internalised.

RLA 4

1 Low self-esteem; eagerness to please and impress people.

2 Addiction to coffee and cigarettes.

3 Voluntary.

RLA 5

1 The relationship is a correlation, so there should be caution about deciding whether smoking in pregnancy causes childhood conduct disorders.

2 There are two main avenues of effect – physiological or psychological. The physiological route is through nicotine in the bloodstream reaching the foetus. Psychologically, smoking may be a symptom of stress and psychological problems in the mother.

3 The other problems may include family relationships, social problems (like housing) or poverty/employment issues.

RLA 6

1a The underlying assumption is that the poorer social classes are the main committers of crime.

 b More abortions by these social classes means less children to commit the crimes.

2 Research with statistical data.

3 Eugenics is the belief that certain groups in society should be sterilised in order to make society a better place. Increased abortions among the poorer social classes is a form of sterilization for these groups.

RLA 7

1 Bob believes that the man at the bar was laughing at him.

2 The violence is justified because the women on the train was 'getting rather stuck up' (that is, he blames the victim).

3 The touching of Bob's wife may have been an accident in a crowded pub, and the man was laughing because he was talking to other people. In fact he may not have realised that he even touched Bob's wife.

RLA 8

1 1 in 2 = 50%; 1 in 5 = 20%; 1 in 6 = 16.66% 1 in 4 = 25%; 1 in 8 = 12.5%.

2 For example, Kanin (1985).

3 A form of the 'just world hypothesis' - people receive what they deserve.

RLA 9

1 **a** Cracker; **b** no.

2 British profilers tend to use data from a large number of crimes to look for patterns, while the Americans based their information on detailed interviews with serial killers in prison.

3 Crime scene analysis; the profiler is looking for specific psychological clues left by the attacher – for example, whether there was a sexual attack before the murder or not; whether the child with the victim was injured or not.

RLA 10

1 The two men were seen at the same truck hire office on the same day.

2 Loftus (1975) study involving the recall of a barn that was not in a film seen earlier.

3 By using questions to establish the context of each observation.

RLA 11

1 The encoding of memories.

2 The witness may recognise a face in the identity parade and not know where the recognition comes from – the 'mugshots' or the crime.

3 These may include: the police saying 'we've found the person', and the police asking 'are you sure?' after a particular choice of suspect.

RLA 12

1 These factors include: if the assault is sexual, if there is stalking involved, if the victim is homeless, and if the victim is already anxious or depressed.

2 Yes. Women are more likely to suffer violence at the hands of someone they know, and for men it is often a stranger.

3 The factors include blame attribution, perceived control or counterfactual thinking.

RLA 13

1 Factual PTP.

2 The judge's instructions to ignore certain information is ineffective. In fact, juries remember more the information they are told to forget.

3 Emotive PTP – that is, assuming guilt before the trial.

RLA 14

1 Psychologically prisoners impose structures in their mind to survive. Thus a small change challenges that whole structure.

2 Just before release many issues that were forgotten throughout the prison sentence become important (like having to find a job in the outside world).

3 'Jail sex' allows prisoners to pretend that they are having sex with a woman. Few of them would admit that it is a homosexual act.

B Selected bibliography

Adlam, KRC (1985). 'The psychological characteristics of police officers.' In Thackrah, JR (ed.) *Contemporary Policing*. London: Sphere Reference.

Aronson, E, Wilson, TD and Akert, RM (1999). *Social Psychology* (third edition). New York: Longman.

Baldwin, J and McConville, M (1979). *Jury Trials*. Oxford: Blackwell and Oxford University Press.

Bartol, CR (1999). *Criminal Behaviour: A Psychosocial Approach* (fifth edition). New Jersey: Prentice Hall.

Black, DA (1982). 'A five year follow-up study of male patients discharged from Broadmoor hospital.' In Gunn, J and Farrington, DP (eds) *Abnormal Offenders, Delinquency and the Criminal Justice System*. Chichester: Wiley.

Blackburn, R (1993). *Psychology of Criminal Conduct*. Chichester: John Wiley.

Blumenthal, S, Gudjonsson, G and Burns, J (1999). 'Cognitive distortions and blame attribution in sex offenders against adults and children.' *Child Abuse and Neglect* 23, 2, pp. 129–43.

Boon, J and Davies, G (1992). 'Fact and fiction in offender profiling issues.' *Legal and Criminological Psychology* 32, pp. 3–9.

Bottoms, AE, Mawby, RI and Xanthos, PD (1981). *Sheffield Study on Urban Social Structure and Crime, Part 3*. London: HMSO.

Bowling, B (1999). 'The rise and fall of New York murder: zero tolerance or crack's decline?' *British Journal of Criminology* 39, 4, pp. 531–54.

Brown, DR, Salmon, K, Pipe, M-E *et al* (1999). 'Children's recall of medical experiences: the impact of stress.' *Child Abuse and Neglect* 23, 3, pp. 209–16.

Buckhout, R (1974). 'Eye witness testimony.' *Scientific American* 231, 6, pp. 23–31.

Bull, R and Barnes, P (1995). 'Children as witnesses.' In Bancroft, D and Carr, T (eds) *Influencing Children's Development*. London: Sage.

Burrows, J (1980). 'Closed circuit television and crime on the London Underground.' In Clarke, RVG and Mayhew, P (eds) *Designing Out Crime*. London: HMSO.

Burton, AM *et al* (1999). 'Face recognition in poor quality video.' *Psychological Sciences* 10, 3, pp. 243–8.

Byers, B, Crider, BW and Biggers, GK (1999). 'Bias crime motivation: a study of hate crime and offender neutralisation techniques used against the Amish.' *Journal of Contemporary Criminal Justice* 15, 1, pp. 78–96.

Canter, D (1994). *Criminal Shadows*. London: HarperCollins.

Canter, D and Heritage, R (1990). 'A multivariate model of sexual offence behaviour: developments in offender profiling.' *Journal of Forensic Psychiatry* 1, pp. 185–212.

Canter, D and Larkin, P (1993). 'The environmental range of serial rapists.' *Journal of Environmental Psychology* 13, pp. 63–9.

Canter, D and Fritzon, K (1998). 'Differentiating arsonists: a model of firesetting actions and characteristics.' *Legal and Criminological Psychology* 3, pp. 73–96.

Carpenter, BN and Raza, SM (1987). 'Personality characteristics of police applicants.' *Journal of Police Science and Administration* 15, p. 16.

Cavadino, M (1998). 'Death to the psychopath.' *Journal of Forensic Psychiatry* 9, 1, pp. 5–8.

Chambers, D (1995). 'What are the facts?' In Jones, D and Barker, P (eds) *Battered Britain*. London: Broadcasting Support Services.

Chapdelaine, A and Griffin, SF (1997). 'Beliefs of guilt and recommended sentence as a function of juror bias in the OJ Simpson trial.' *Journal of Social Issues* 53, 3, pp. 477–85.

Clarke, RV (1997) (ed.). *Situational Crime Prevention: Successful Case Studies* (second edition). Albany, NY: Harrow and Heston.

Copson, G (1995). 'Coals to Newcastle?' *Police*

Research Group Special Interest Series: Paper 7. London: Home Office Police Dept.

Cornish, DB and Clarke, RVG (1986) (eds). *The Reasoning Criminal: Rational Choice Perspectives.* New York: Springer-Verlag.

Cowley, G (1993). 'The not-young and the restless.' *Newsweek* 26/7, pp. 48–9.

Crawford, A (1998). *Crime Prevention and Community Safety.* London: Longman.

Croyle, RT and Loftus, E (1994). 'Psychology and law.' In Colman, A (ed.) *Controversies in Psychology.* London: Longman.

Dalteg, A and Levander, S (1998). '12,000 crimes by 75 boys.' *Journal of Forensic Psychiatry* 9, 1, pp. 39–57.

Davies, A (1997). 'Specific profile analysis: a data-based approach to offender profiling.' In Jackson, JL and Bekerian, DA (eds) *Offender Profiling: Theory, Research and Practice.* Chichester: John Wiley.

Davies, GM and Noon, E (1991). *An Evaluation of the Live Link for Child Witnesses.* London: Home Office.

Davies, G, Wilson, C, Mitchell, R and Milsom, J (1995). *Videotaping Children's Evidence: An Evaluation.* London: Home Office.

Dent, H and Flin, R (1992) (eds). *Children Witnesses.* Chichester: Wiley.

Di Fazio, R, Kroner, DG and Forth, AE (1997). 'The Attribution of Blame Scale with an incarcerated sample: factor structure, reliability and validity.' *Criminal Behaviour and Mental Health* 7, pp. 153–64.

Donnellan, C (1999). *Dealing with Domestic Violence.* Cambridge: Independence.

Farrington, DP (1995). 'The development of offending and anti-social behaviour from childhood.' *Journal of Child Psychology and Psychiatry* 36, 6, pp. 924–64.

Farrington, DP and West, DJ (1990). 'The Cambridge study in delinquent development: a long term follow up of 411 London males.' In Kaiser, G and Kerner, HJ (eds) *Criminal: Personality, Behaviour, Life History.* Heidelberg: Springer-Verlag.

FBI (1985). 'Crime scene and profile characteristics of organized and disorganised murderers.' *FBI Law Enforcement Bulletin* 54, 8, 18–25.

Feldman, RS (1998). *Social Psychology* (fourth edition). Englewood Cliffs, NJ: Prentice Hall.

Fisher, RP, Geiselman, RE and Raymond, DS (1987). 'Critical analysis of police interview techniques.' *Journal of Police Science and Administration* 15, pp. 177–85.

Friendship, C: McClintock, T, Rutter, S and Maden, A (1999). 'Re-offending: patients discharged from a Regional Secure Unit.' *Criminal Behaviour and Mental Health* 9, pp. 226–36.

Furnham, AF and Thompson, J (1991). 'Personality and self-reported delinquency.' *Personality and Individual Differences* 12, pp. 585–93.

Gee, S, Gregory, M and Pipe, M-E (1999). '"What colour is your pet dinosaur?" The impact of pre-interview training and question type on children's answers.' *Legal and Criminological Psychology* 4, pp. 111–28.

Geiselman, RE, Fisher, RP, MacKinnon, DP and Holland, HL (1985). 'Eye-witness memory enhancement in police interview: cognitive retrieval mnemonics vs hypnosis.' *Journal of Applied Psychology* 70, pp. 401–12.

Gibbs, WW (1995). 'Seeking the criminal element.' *Scientific American* March, pp. 76–83.

Giddens, A (1997). *Sociology* (third edition). Cambridge: Polity Press.

Goodman, GS, Taub, E, Jones, D, England, P, Port, P, Rudy, L and Prado-Estrade, L (1992). 'Emotional effects of criminal court testimony on child sexual assault victims.' *Monographs of Society for Research on Child Development* 57, 5.

Grubin, D (1995). 'Offender Profiling.' *Journal of Forensic Psychiatry* 6, 2, pp. 259–63.

Gudjonsson, GH (1984). 'Attribution of blame for criminal acts and its relationship with personality.' *Personality and Individual Differences* 5, pp. 53–8.

Gudjonsson, GH (1985). 'Psychological evidence in court: results from BPS survey.' *Bulletin of the British Psychological Society* 38, pp. 327–30.

Gudjonsson, GH (1990). 'Self-deception and other-deception in forensic assessment.' *Personality and Individual Differences* 11, pp. 219–25.

Gudjonsson, GH (1991). 'The effects of intelligence and memory on group differences in suggestibility and compliance.' *Personality and Individual Differences* 12, pp. 503–505.

Gudjonsson, GH (1992). 'Psychology of

Interrogations', *Confessions and Testimony*. Chichester: Wiley.

Gudjonsson, GH (1995). '"I'll help you boys as much as I can": how eagerness to please can result in a false confession.' *Journal Of Forensic Psychiatry* 6, 2, pp. 333–42.

Gudjonsson, GH (1999). 'The making of a serial false confessor: the confessions of Henry Lee Lucas.' *Journal of Forensic Psychiatry* 10, 2, pp. 416–26.

Gudjonsson, GH and Adlam, KRC (1983). 'Personality patterns of British Police Officers.' *Personality and Individual Differences* 4, 5, pp. 507–12.

Gudjonsson, GH and MacKeith, JAC (1982). 'False confession, psychological effects of interrogation: a discussion paper.' In Trankell, A (ed.) *Reconstructing the Past: The Role of Psychologists in Criminal Trials*. Deventer, Holland: Kluwer.

Gudjonsson, GH and Petursson, H (1991). 'Custodial interrogation: why do suspects confess and how does it relate to their crimes, attitude and personality.' *Personality and Individual Differences* 12, pp. 295–306.

Hall, P (1995). 'Can we plan away crime?' In Jones, D and Barker, P (eds) *Battered Britain*. London: Channel 4 TV.

Hanewicz, MB (1978). 'Police personality: a Jungian perspective.' *Journal of Crime and Delinquency* 24, pp. 152–72.

Hare, D (1970). *Psychopathy: Theory and Research*. New York: Wiley.

Hare, D (1980). 'A research scale for assessment of psychopathy in criminal populations.' *Personality and Individual Differences* 1, pp. 111–19.

Hare, D (1991). *The Hare Psychopathy Checklist–Revised*. Toronto: Multi-Health Systems.

Harrower, J (1998). *Applying Psychology to Crime*. London: Hodder and Stoughton.

Hastie, R, Penrod, SD and Pennington, N (1983). *Inside the Jury*. Cambridge: Harvard University Press.

Hayes, BK and Delamothe, K (1997). 'Cognitive interview procedures and suggestibility in children's recall.' *Journal of Applied Psychology* 82, 4, pp. 562–77.

Hickey, E (1991). *Serial Murderers and their Victims*. Belmont: Wadsworth.

Hollin, CR (1989). *Psychology and Crime*. London: Routledge.

Hollin, CR (1992). *Criminal Behaviour*. London: Falmer Press.

Hollin, C (1997). 'Adolescent predictors of adult offending.' *Psychology Review* April, pp. 21–5.

Holmes, RM (1989). *Profiling Violent Crimes: An Investigative Tool*. Newbury Park, CA: Sage.

Holmes, R and DeBurger, J (1988). *Serial Murder*. Newbury Park: Sage.

Home Office (1992). *Memorandum of Good Practice on Video Interviews with Child Witnesses for Criminal Proceedings*. London: HMSO.

Hough, M and Mayhew, P (1983). *The British Crime Survey: 1st Report*. London: HMSO.

Hough, M and Mayhew, P (1985). 'Taking Account of Crime: Key Findings' from second *British Crime Survey*. London: HMSO.

Inch, H, Rowlands, P and Soliman, A (1995). 'Deliberate self-harm in a young offenders' institution.' *Journal of Forensic Psychiatry* 6, 1, pp. 161–72.

Kalven, J and Zeisel, H (1966). *American Jury*. Boston: Little, Brown.

Kassin, SM and Wrightsman, LS (1983). 'The construction and validation of a juror bias scale.' *Journal of Research in Personality* 17, pp. 423–42.

Kassin, SM and Wrightsman, LS (1988). *The American Jury on Trial: Psychological Perspectives*. New York: Hemisphere.

Kohnken, G (1996). 'Social psychology and law.' In Semin, GR and Fiedler, K (eds) *Applied Social Psychology*. London: Sage.

Loftus, EF (1975). 'Leading questions and eye witness report.' *Cognitive Psychology* 7, pp. 560–72.

Loftus, EF (1979). 'Reactions to blatantly contradictory information.' *Memory and Cognition* 7, pp. 368–74.

Loftus, EF (1996). *Eyewitness Testimony* (second edition). Cambridge, Mass: Harvard University Press.

Loftus, EF, Manber, M and Keating, JP (1983). 'Recollection of naturalistic events: context enhancement vs negative cueing.' *Human Learning* 3, pp. 83–92.

Loftus, EF, Loftus, GR and Messo, J (1987). 'Some facts about "weapon focus".' *Law and Human Behaviour* 11, pp. 55–62.

McCabe, S and Purves, R (1974). *The Shadow Jury at Work*. Oxford: Blackwell.

McClintock, T (1997). 'Is the jury trial a lottery?' *Journal of Forensic Psychiatry* 8, 1, pp. 118–26.

Maguire, M and Corbett, C (1987). *The Effects of Crime and Work of Victim Support Schemes*. Aldershot: Gower.

Mahoney, B and Dixon, J (1997). 'A fair and just system.' *Psychology Review* November, pp. 30–32.

Mawby, RI and Gill, ML (1987). *Crime Victims*. London: Tavistock Publications.

Mayhew, P, Elliott, D and Dowd, L (1989). *The 1988 British Crime Survey*. London: HMSO.

Memon, A, Wark, L, Bull, R and Koehnken, G (1997). 'Isolating the effects of cognitive interview techniques.' *British Journal of Psychology* 88, pp. 179–97.

Mirrlees-Black, C; Mayhew, P and Percy, A (1996). *The 1996 British Crime Survey*. London: HMSO.

Mirrlees-Black, C, Budd, T, Patridge, S and Mayhew, P (1998). *The 1998 British Crime Survey*. London: HMSO.

Mitchell, KJ, Livosky, M and Mather, M (1998). 'The weapon focus effect revisited: the role of novelty.' *Legal and Criminological Psychology* 3, pp. 287–303.

Moffitt, TE (1993). 'Adolescent-limited and life-course-persistent anti-social behaviour: a developmental taxonomy.' *Psychological Review* 100, pp. 674–701.

Moir, A and Jessel, D (1995). *A Mind to Crime*. London: Michael Joseph.

Morgan, H and Thomas, K (1996). A psychodynamic perspective on group processes.' In Wetherell, M (ed.) *Identities, Groups and Social Issues*. London: Sage.

Novaco, RW (1975). *Anger Control: The Development and Evaluation of an Experimental Treatment*. Lexington: DC Heath.

O'Block, RL, Donnermeyer, JF and Doeren, SE (1991). *Security and Crime Prevention* (second edition). Boston: Butterworth-Heinemann.

Padawer-Singer, AM and Barton, A (1974). 'The impact of pre-trial publicity on jurors' verdicts.' In Simon, RJ (ed.) *The Jury System in USA: A Critical Overview*. Beverly Hills, Ca: Sage.

Palmer, EJ and Hollin, CR (1998). 'A comparison of patterns of moral development in young offenders and non-offenders.' *Legal and Criminological Psychology* 3, pp. 225–35.

Peacock, MJ, Cowan, G, Bommersbach, M, Smith, SY and Stahly, G (1997). 'Pre-trial predictors of judgments in the OJ Simpson case.' *Journal of Social Issues* 53, 3, pp. 441–52.

Pearse, J and Gudjonsson, GH (1999). 'Measuring influential police interviewing tactics: a factor-analytic approach.' *Legal and Criminological Psychology* 4, pp. 221–38.

Pennington, N and Hastie, R (1990). 'Practical implications of psychological research on juror and jury decision-making.' *Personality and Social Psychology Bulletin* 16, pp. 90–105.

Ressler, RK, Burgess, AW and Douglas, J (1984). *Sexual Homicide: Patterns and Motives*. Lexington: Lexington Books.

Riordan, S (1999). 'Indecent exposure: the impact upon the victim's fear of sexual crime.' *Journal of Forensic Psychiatry* 10, 2, pp. 309–16.

Robinson, F, Keithley, J, Robinson, S and Childs, S (1998). 'Exploring the Impacts of Crime on Health and Health Services: A Feasibility Study.' University of Durham: Dept of Sociology and Social Policy.

Rossmo, DK (1997). 'Geographic profiling.' In Jackson, JL and Bekerian, DA (eds) *Offender Profiling: Theory, Research and Practice*. Chichester: John Wiley.

Sabini, J (1995). *Social Psychology* (second edition). New York: WW Norton and Co.

Sapsford, R (1996). 'Domains of analysis.' In Sapsford, R (ed.) *Issues for Social Psychology*. Milton Keynes: Open University.

Shapiro, P and Penrod, SD (1986). 'A meta-analysis of facial identification studies.' *Psychological Bulletin* 100, pp. 139–56.

Shine, J and Hobson, J (1997). 'Construct validity of the Hare Psychopathy Checklist, Revised, on a UK prison population.' *Journal of Forensic Psychiatry* 8, 3, pp. 546–61.

Social Services Inspectorate (1994). *The Child, the Court and the Video*. Heywood. Lancs: DoH.

Solomon, GS and Ray, JB (1984). 'Irrational beliefs of shoplifters.' *Journal of Clinical Psychology* 40, pp. 1075–7.

Spencer, JR and Flin, R (1993). *Evidence of Children* (second edition). London: Blackstone.

Stahly, GB and Walker, LEA (1997). 'What are nice feminists like you doing on the OJ Simpson defense team?' *Journal of Social Issues* 53, 3, pp. 425–39.

Stanko, E (1990). 'When precaution is normal: a feminist critique of crime prevention.' In Gelsthorpe, L and Morris, A (eds) *Feminist Perspectives in Criminology*. Milton Keynes: Open University Press.

Steels, M, Rony, G, Larkin, E, Jones, P, Croudace, T and Duggan, C (1998). 'Discharged from special hospital under restrictions: a comparison of the fates of psychopaths and the mentally ill.' *Criminal Behaviour and Mental Health* 8, pp. 39–56.

Stephenson, GM (1992). *The Psychology of the Criminal Justice System*. Oxford: Blackwell.

Topp, DO (1999). 'Suicide in prisons.' *British Journal of Psychiatry* 134, pp. 24–7.

Towl, G (1999). 'Self-inflicted deaths in prisons in England and Wales from 1988 to 1996.' *British Journal of Forensic Psychiatry* 1, 2, pp. 28–33.

Tversky, A and Kahneman, D (1981). 'The framing of decisions and the psychology of choice.' *Science*, 30 January.

Wansell, G (1996). *An Evil Love: The Life of Frederick West*. London: Hodder Headline.

Welsh, BC and Farrington, DP (1999). 'Value for money?' *British Journal of Criminology* 39, 3, pp. 345–68.

Wetherell, M and Maybin, J (1996). 'The distributed self: a social constructionist perspective.' In Stevens, R (ed.) *Understanding the Self*. London: Sage.

Wilson, S (1980). 'Vandalism and "defensible space" on London housing estates.' In Clarke, RVG and Mayhew, P (eds) *Designing Out Crime*. London: HMSO.

Women's Unit (1999). *Living Without Fear*. London: HMSO.

Worsley, K (1998). 'Close-circuit cameras short-circuit justice.' *Times Higher Educational Supplement*.

Radio

All in the Mind (1991). Graham Davies; 'Can you tell if someone is lying?' 22/10; BBC Radio 4.

All in the Mind (1992). James MacKeith; 'Why do people make false confessions?' 27/5; BBC Radio 4.

All in the Mind (1996). Carol Sheldrick; 28/5; BBC Radio 4.

Laying Down the Law (1995). 'Banged up.' BBC Radio 5.

Laying Down the Law (1995). 'Lady be good.' BBC Radio 5.

Laying Down the Law (1995). Michael Lyons; 'Criminals: Born or made?' BBC Radio 5.

Mind Matters (1993). 'Psychology of crime.' BBC World Service.

Science Now (1991). Graham Davies; 23/4; BBC Radio 4.

Science Now (1995). Michael Rutter; 18/2; BBC Radio 4.

Science Now (1996). Graham Davies; 20/8; BBC Radio 4.

Science Now (1997). Hayden Ellis; 27/12; BBC Radio 4.

Television

A Mind to Crime (1996). 'The dangerous few.' Channel 4.

A Mind to Crime (1996). Debate; Stephen Rose; Channel 4.

A Mind to Crime (1996). 'Violent minds.' Channel 4.

CNN Presents (1996). 'Born bad.' CNNI.

Discovery Magazine (1999). 'Victims of memory.' Discovery Channel.

Horizon (1993). 'Wot U lookin' at.' 24/5; BBC.

Inside Story (1999). 'The Russian cracker.' BBC.

Mind Machine (1989). 'The violent mind.' BBC.

TimeWatch (1996). 'Bad boys.' BBC.

Viewpoint '93 (1993). 'Murder in mind.' ITV.

* Complete references can be obtained from the publishers.

Index